Professional
Coach
Training

Professional Coach Training

A COACHING4TODAY'S LEADERS TEXTBOOK

By J. Val Hastings, MCC, and Trigena H. Halley, PCC

<u>Contact Information</u>

Val – 1.877.381.2672, val@coaching4todaysleaders.com
Trigena – 1.801.915.4046, trigena@me.com

<u>Web Site</u>
www.coaching4todaysleaders.com

ISBN #978-0-9886128-6-0

Published in the USA

Table of Contents

Continued on next page...

Continued from previous page...

RESOURCES

Acknowledgments—J. Val Hastings

This book is dedicated to those who have empowered me as a person, a pastor, a leader and a professional coach.

To my wife, Wendy, who continually encourages me to pursue my dreams! Thank you for your support and encouragement. What a gift you have given me. I love you.

To my parents, Val Sr., and Audrey Hastings, who were my first real coaches. Thank you for empowering me in the ways that you parented me. Thank you for bringing out the best in me and for seeing more in me than I saw in myself at times.

To my father, Val Sr., who modeled and mentored me in leadership. Thank you for the many, many hours we spoke of leadership and how to best empower others. I benefited much from our time together.

To my two daughters, Bryanna and Shelby, my sources of pride and joy. I love being your father.

To my Mentor-Coach and friend Ken Abrams, MCC. Over the years Ken has contributed much to my coaching mastery. Thanks for honing my coaching skills.

To the Coaching4Today'sLeaders Faculty and Trainers who have contributed to this book and provided me with valuable feedback.

To all of the professions that I have coached. This book is filled with what you have taught me. Others will benefit from you.

Acknowledgments—Trigena H. Halley

This book is dedicated to those who have supported and believed in me as a person and as a professional coach.

To my husband, Steve, who supported me in pursuing my passions, and has encouraged me to live out my dream. Thanks for always keeping me centered and never giving me the answer.

To my wonderful children, Ethan and Addison, what a joy it is to have you in my life and watch you grow. God has blessed me with your presence and I learn from you daily!

To the coaches in my life—Karen Hill, Karla Marshall, Dr. Diane Menendez, MCC, and Val Hastings, MCC. Thanks for listening, teaching and helping me discover who I am as a wife, mom, leader and coach! Your support and, most of all, your friendship has shaped who I am today.

To those of you who I "live life with" (you know who you are Kelly, Beth Ann, and Tonia). Thanks for being adventurous with me and encouraging me to chase after all my dreams and goals. You are each amazing women who make a difference in the lives of others on a daily basis – thanks for adding value to mine!

To all organizations and leaders I have coached. Thanks for allowing me to work with you—I am grateful to have crossed your path!

Introduction

You may be wondering why a former pastor (Val) and a business person (Trigena) would team up together to write a book on coaching. Our belief is that most organizations and churches have much in common in terms of supporting the growth and development of individuals. To that end, the goal is to support those leaders that are seeking ways to inspire, empower, and develop individuals and teams to perform at peak performance and get sustainable results that matter.

Using coaching as a leadership tool is one way to get results and empower others, not only as leaders of organizations, but also within faith-based communities. The coaching skills contained in this textbook will help leaders everywhere gain greater clarity about how to empower others, as well as get results and impact productivity.

Whether you are a first time leader or a CEO, coaching is an extremely valuable and useful tool. At its core, coaching is about empowering others and, when individuals are empowered, achievement of the vision begins to emerge.

Whatever (or whoever) motivated you to learn more about coaching, I want to thank you for taking this step. You are beginning a journey that will add tremendously to your life and the lives of others.

Congratulations! Let's begin.

Chapter One

Getting Started as a Coach

WHAT IS COACHING?

When people discover I am coach, they usually ask me what coaching is. As I start to explain, I usually observe a combination of confusion and intrigue in the listener's expression. Coaching, while powerful and transformational, is hard for many to understand. One person has said she believes the real reason people hire me as their coach is because they like the way my voice sounds on the phone. Others have hired me as their coach saying, "I don't know what coaching is, but whatever you did for _____ (another leader), I want you to do for me." Or they have hired me to be a sounding board and someone who they can be accountable to as they move forward toward new behaviors, changes and/or goals.

It is always fun to hear the responses to the explanation of coaching: "So you're going to do lots of listening, you're not going to tell me what to do, nor are you going to try to fix me. I'm going to do all the work AND I'm going to pay you!"

Over the years I have discovered that the best way to help someone understand coaching is to give them a firsthand experience. That's why I conduct a LIVE coaching demonstration at the beginning of every coach training event I facilitate. Next, I invite the participants to define what coaching is, based on what they have just witnessed. Another way to help others understand coaching is to offer a complimentary coaching session to individuals and leaders who are considering using a coach. This is a great way to help someone understand the power of coaching.

And so, in addition to reading this manual, I invite you to experience your own demonstration of coaching by scheduling a complimentary coaching session. Not only is that the best way to understand coaching, you will also benefit from being coached. (Please contact us to schedule your complimentary session with no strings attached.)

Let's define what coaching is and what it is not. The International Coach Federation (www.coachfederation.org) defines coaching as "partnering with clients in a thought-provoking and creative process that inspires them to maximize their personal and professional potential."

Here is how I define coaching: As a coach, I help people get the results they want by bringing out the best in them. Coaching isn't about fixing people or solving problems; coaching is a developmental or discovery-based process. Similar to athletic coaches, I further develop the skill and talent already inherent in the people I coach.

Whether you use the International Coach Federation definition of coaching, our definition, or develop your own, there are several key components to highlight:

1. Coaching is a partnership.

The coach and the coachee are involved in a collaborative process that is 100% about the person being coached. The relationship between the coach and coachee is of utmost importance. Safety and trust in this relationship create an environment in which fresh perspectives and new ways of working, leading and being are explored. Coachees are more likely to let you see who they really are if they believe that they can trust you.

2. Coaching accelerates what is already underway or about to begin.

This is a key distinction between coaching and other disciplines. Because the perspective is that the person is already whole and complete, I'm not moving immediately into fix-it mode or bringing a scarcity mentality. Instead, I look for clues and dig for treasures in what I see in front of me. Coaches enjoy spending time at the intersection of curiosity and wonder.

Many of the individuals and teams I coach initially have little or no awareness of what is already underway or about to begin. One of the benefits of the coaching process is that it creates space in the coachee's schedule—even if it's only 30 minutes—to step back and see what is. Through deep listening and powerful questions, the coach helps the other person gain greater clarity about what they really want, as well as clarity about what needs to occur going forward.

3. Coaches maximize potential, moving people from good to great.

Coaches do more than inspire or cheer-on; coaches help people develop and actually make forward progress. Have you ever heard of an Olympic athlete who achieved any success without coaching? A coach will develop you further, faster and deeper than you could ever do on your own.

One of the ways I maximize coaching is by tapping into the greatness of those I coach. Coaches intentionally look for and develop the strengths and giftedness of the person being coached. Benjamin Zander explains this in his book *The Art of Possibility*. Zander begins each term by informing his students they already have an "A." Our coachees also begin with an "A." (We'll talk a little more about Ben Zander later in this book.)

One of the best examples of beginning with an "A" is how I develop and nurture future leaders in our organizations. Most young leaders go into meetings with clients, prospective clients and internal teams hoping to add value, get results and move their organization ahead. Leaders, who have coaches who believe in their capabilities, expect great things and give them their "A," have an added advantage. When I work with future leaders, I support them in developing solutions and being accountable to results, and then step back and allow them the freedom to achieve those accomplishments.

Another way that coaches maximize potential is by looking beyond solutions to shifts. Shift work involves internal perspectives, beliefs and assumptions. As a coach, I "shine a flashlight" on their perspectives, beliefs, and assumptions, and help them see how these support and limit their forward progress. Let me give you an example. When I started training for my first half-marathon, I jokingly referred to myself as a "non-runner who runs." I steadily moved my mileage upward but got "stuck" at the six-mile range and couldn't move past it. As I was working with another coach, he asked "what is the relationship between the belief you are a non-runner and your lack of moving forward?" It was during that conversation that I became acutely aware of how my belief was keeping me from moving forward. I changed my belief and I changed my thinking, which in turn changed how I viewed myself and my capabilities.

Many years ago I had a belief that I was "just a pastor" and no one would hire a pastor as their coach—especially in the business world. There were no external solutions or action plans that could adequately address this internal belief. Instead, my coach at the time helped me create an awareness of how this internal belief was limiting me, plus my coach helped me gain an entirely new perspective on this belief. All of a sudden I just knew that there were people who would want to hire me as their coach because I was a pastor. That was all I needed. A giant leap forward followed.

Another way that coaches maximize the potential of coachees is to walk beside them, rather than trying to lead them. The coachee remains in the driver's seat, but the coach is invited along for the ride. A coach is not a "sage on the stage, but a guide alongside." How true! We fully help others develop their potential, but not by doing for them or telling them what to do. In this role of "guide alongside," the coach becomes:

- Your partner in achieving professional and personal goals.

- Your sounding board when making decisions.

- Your support in professional and personal development.

- Your guide in communication and life skills.

- Your motivation when strong actions are needed.

- Your unconditional supporter when you take a hit.

How is Coaching Different from Therapy, Consulting and Mentoring?

Coaching is not the "be all and end all" of helping people. While there are tremendous benefits to coaching, the same is true of therapy, consulting and mentoring. All are of value. Taking that a step further, it is absolutely essential that we, as coaches, appreciate the important contributions therapists, consultants and mentors make to the ongoing success of those we coach. In fact, many of those I coach are also using the services of a therapist, consultant or mentor.

There is much overlap between coaching and therapy, consulting, and mentoring. Consultants identify with the brainstorming, designing the plan, and follow-through elements of the coaching process, while mentors relate to our "guide alongside" philosophy. During a recent coach training event for therapists, a participant stated that many of the listening concepts and skills he was learning were very similar to what he learned as a therapist. Another marriage and family therapist defined coaching as "therapy for healthy people" and declared how refreshing it would be to work with people who were basically whole and complete.

Many coaches see the benefits of combining coaching with these other modalities. A perfect example is the mentor-coaching I offer coaches. Those I mentor-coach benefit from the access I have to both mentoring and coaching skills and techniques. Sometimes I blend the two; other times I use one or the other. There are also many consultants and therapists who now blend coaching into their practices. It is very important to clearly understand the similarities and differences when intentionally overlapping coaching with another discipline or skill set. The key is to know which discipline will yield the best results for the coachee, not which is easiest or fastest for the coach.

Coaching is still new enough that there are many competing perceptions about what it is. Someone who offers coaching may or may not be adhering to the techniques and approaches you are learning here. I have heard, on more than one occasion, how someone's "coach" does a great job giving "advice" and "telling them what to do." They are often taken aback when they are introduced to my process. It takes a bit of time to untrain them and then retrain them on the true coaching process. The good news is that, after experiencing coaching, most individuals prefer it and see the merits of the coaching process.

Coaching Versus Therapy

Over the years, several key distinctions between coaching and therapy have been discovered. One distinction is that therapy is about recovery, while coaching is about discovery. For the most part, therapy is about recovering from a pain or dysfunction, often arising from the past. The focus is on recovering overall psychological health.

Coaching, on the other hand, assumes an overall level of health and wellness and, therefore, isn't focused on recovery, but rather on discovery. The coaching process happens in an environment of curiosity and wonder as I seek peak performance in those I coach. Using a timeline, therapy is usually recovering from the past and bringing the person into a healthy present. Coaches begin in the healthy present and launch out to create and discover the future.

Another helpful distinction is archaeology versus architecture. Therapy, like archaeology, digs into the past to put the present into context. Coaching, similar to architecture, focuses on designing, creating and supporting the future. I often remind new coaches that unless there is forward progress, or signs that forward progress is coming, it's not really coaching.

One more distinction: therapy versus therapeutic. Many individuals and groups report the therapeutic benefits of coaching; they generally feel more positive about themselves, as well as their present and future, as a result of coaching. Yes! It feels good to really make progress and actually accomplish what you set out to accomplish. Coaching is therapeutic, but it's not therapy. Those who coach have an ethical obligation to make referrals for therapy when needed. Indicators may include:

- An increase in overall sadness
- Difficulty focusing
- Changes in sleep patterns, appetite and anger
- Feelings of hopelessness
- An increase of risk-taking behavior

- Thoughts of suicide

- Intense focus on past

Coaching versus Consulting

There are two questions that come to my mind when I consider the distinction between coaching and consulting:

- Who is the recognized expert?

- Who is responsible for the outcome?

> *Sometimes the biggest contribution a coach can make to another person is three simple words: "I don't know." It is by being open to not knowing that a coach propels the coachee forward.*

In consulting, the recognized expert is the consultant. Most people work with a consultant because they believe the consultant's expertise will benefit them and their organization. Usually the consultant helps diagnose problems and prescribes a set of solutions. In coaching, the recognized expert is the person or team being coached. The coaching perspective is that coachees are capable of generating their own solutions. The role of the coach is to provide a discovery-based framework that taps further into the expertise of the person being coached.

As far as who is responsible for the outcome, in consulting, the consultant is responsible for the desired outcome. By following the consultant's advice, their client will achieve the desired outcome. Contrast this with coaching. Coaches seek to empower the one being coached. It is the coachee doing the work who is responsible for the outcome; they generate their own plans and take their own actions. The coach is responsible for holding the framework of the coaching process, but not for the outcome.

Coaching versus Mentoring

Mentoring is a process of guiding another along a path that the mentor has already traveled. The sharing or guidance includes perspectives and learning from the mentor's own experience. The underlying premise is that the insight and guidance of the mentor can accelerate the learning curve of the one being mentored. Although in many instances a coach and coachee might share a similar experience, it is not the coach's personal or professional experience that is of greatest value. In the coaching relationship, it is the coachee's experiences which are of most importance.

Does the coach ever share their experiences or expertise? At a recent workshop at an International Coach Federation (ICF) conference, the top ten things that coachees value from their coach were highlighted. Number seven on the list was when the coach shares advice and experience when asked for and when appropriate. Notice those qualifiers— when asked for and when appropriate.

When coachees come right out and ask me to tell them what to do, I usually preface any reply by saying something like "Based on those I have coached in a similar situation, here are a few ideas. What do you think?" In other words, I'm holding my advice lightly and going back into coaching mode once the advice is offered. As coaches we must remember that it's only our best-guess opinion and nothing more.

When is it appropriate to share experiences and expertise? Sometimes the person I am coaching may be genuinely stuck and offering advice may serve to prime the pump and get them thinking. Another time may be when a bigger goal can be met more quickly and effectively, if they can leap over things of lesser importance. In all of these cases, though, it is presumed you have already established a coaching relationship of trust and safety, and you are both clear that this is only your opinion.

Initially, we recommend new coaches refrain from offering advice. Most people have learned how to offer advice in ways that are not helpful and, in fact, disempower others. First, we must learn how not to give advice. Then, we can begin to learn anew the art of advising. I'll talk more about this later in the book.

What Does a Typical Coaching Session Look Like?

An example of coaching a leader who is "stuck" might look like the following:

"We're stuck! We've tried everything and nothing seems to work. We have the BIG picture… but can't seem to get started. The result is that we're losing momentum. It feels like we're taking one step forward, two steps back. Organizational leaders and clients are bailing. I'm beginning to question my ability to lead. Help!"

A coach might employ one of these five strategies:

1. **Ask the leader to tell you more.** One of the best places to begin is to simply invite the person to share further.

2. **Mirror back what you are hearing and observing.** It is amazing how helpful the simple act of mirroring can work. For the coachee, it is very beneficial to hear what they are saying from an outside perspective and how they are being heard.

3. **Invite the leader to describe the vision or BIG picture.** In this scenario the leader states

that "We have the BIG picture...but can't seem to get started." As the coach, confirm they really do have the BIG picture. Over and over again, leaders think they have the BIG picture when they really don't. As a next step, encourage this leader to facilitate more conversation about the vision. The group may have been too quick to move into strategy mode and really needs to hang out a bit more with the vision.

4. **Ask about the plan.** This could very well be an implementation issue. It's not uncommon to develop a wonderful vision, hang it on the wall and assume it will just happen. A vision needs a plan. One of the top reasons a vision is never implemented is that it lacks a plan or the plan is poorly communicated.

5. **Ask about their support system.** Who can help them with this? In addition to a coach, other team members, colleagues and peers can be of tremendous assistance. Likely, there are numerous colleagues who have valuable insights and have learned from similar experiences. Tap into their experiences or seek them out as a sounding board and for an encouraging word.

What Do You Mean by a "Coaching Approach" to Leadership?

A growing number of today's leaders are pursuing coach training as a way of enhancing their ability to lead, as well as a tool for developing individuals and teams. Many leaders view coaching as a tangible way to address their role as a "developer of organizational talent." Coach training offers practical, proven tools and skills that equip leaders to build bench strength, achieve results, enhance performance and empower others.

One way to incorporate coaching into leadership is by coaching groups and teams instead of taking a more traditional leadership approach. Use your coaching skills to help these teams gain clarity about their goals, then get out of their way and let them make it happen. What is the result of this coach approach to leading a team? You get a more effective team whose members are working from their strengths, rather than from your advice. Another way leaders use coaching is individually with their direct reports as a way to support problem solving and accountability to results. Lastly, many organizations are weaving coaching into how they conduct performance reviews and ensure execution of training programs.

> Xerox Corporation carried out several studies on coaching. They determined that in the absence of follow-up coaching to their training classes, 87% of the skills change brought about by the program was lost."
> —Business Wire

As you supervise and evaluate others, imagine giving them an "A" before they even start. How much more empowering would that organizational culture be? Add to that powerful questions and deep listening, and you have a recipe for success!

Our organizations are filled with people experiencing professional and personal transition, who can greatly benefit from the coach approach of support, clarity and accountability. Imagine leaders that cultivate a culture of support and trust, with a skill for bringing out the best in others. Professional transformation, peak performance, and results are bound to follow.

Recently a new coach said she believed coaching was really a luxury for those in leadership, especially in this economy. My response was that effective leadership is not a luxury, but a necessity. Imagine the difference in your organization if you partnered with a coach whose sole purpose was to bring out the very best in you and to help you to continually perform at peak level. If our organizations are going to be successful, then coaching must not be seen as a luxury, but rather as a necessity.

THE FIVE STEP COACHING MODEL

Years ago, as a new coach, one of the most helpful tools for me was a coaching model. The following coaching model will provide you with a framework you can come back to over and over again as your coaching skills progress and as you coach more diverse and interesting people and situations.

Solid coaching, like a solid house, has a:

- **Foundation**
  - Listen
  - Evoke
- **Supportive Frame**
  - Clarify
  - Brainstorm
- **Strong Covering**
  - Support

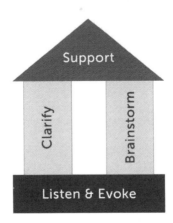

Laying the foundation

Step 1: Listen

The goal as a coach is to listen so closely to your coachee that the answers come out. The ideal ratio is that you are listening 80% of the time and responding 20% of the time. It is absolutely critical that the client feel fully understood. Listen deeply by using these suggestions:

- Listen not just with your ears, but with your eyes and your whole being ("gut-level" listening).

- Listen to the tone, inflection, rate and pitch.

- Listen to what is being said, as well as to what is not being said.

- Pay particular attention to the last thing that is said.

- Listen without judgment, criticism or agenda.

- Listen without thinking about what you will be saying next.

Step 2: Evoke

Prompt the coachee to say more. Evoking is like opening the tap on the sink spigot. You are attempting to get beyond the initial surface and move to the good stuff—the source of the issue.

Examples of evocative responses:

- Hmmmm.

- What else do you want to say about this?

- Tell me more.

- What more should I know?

Propping Up the Supports

Step 3: Clarify

Once the coachee has shared and has actively engaged with you, it's important to respond and clarify what is being said. This offers the coachee an opportunity to hear what they have just verbalized from a slightly different perspective. It also ensures that you and the coachee are on the same page.

Examples of clarifying techniques:

- I heard you say… (mirroring)
- I sense that… (paraphrasing or reflecting back)
- Is this what you mean? (verifying)
- On a scale of 1 to 10, how committed are you to this? 1 = not important, 10 = important (rating)
- Number these things based on which is most important to you. 1 = least important, 10 = most important (ranking)

Step 4: Brainstorm

Once there is clarity about the topic at hand, you and the coachee can now begin to go below the surface and further discuss the issue. Questions are central to the coaching process.

A few examples of questions include:

- What are the options here? Let's list them all.
- What's the simplest solution? What's the craziest solution?
- What's the payoff of NOT dealing with this?
- What's stopping you?
- What do you want to be able to say about this situation three months from now that you can't say today?
- What do you really, REALLY want?

A more complete list of questions is found in the section about powerful questions later in this book.

Providing a Cover

Step 5: Support

Action is central to the coaching experience. Supporting the coachee to design an action step helps move the coachee forward, closing the gap between where they currently are and where they want to be.

A typical coaching conversation might end like this:

- Based on our conversation today, what action would you like to take? When will it be completed?

- What do you want to report back to me at our next coaching session?

- What will bring you closer to your goal?

- What do you need to do in order to focus on this over the next week?

- What will get in the way?

- Who can help you with this?

In subsequent coaching sessions, you'll follow up by asking questions such as:

- What did you accomplish?

- What didn't you accomplish that you said you would?

- What got in the way?

- What's next?

INITIAL CONTACT WITH A NEW COACHEE

This section will cover your initial contact with a coachee or potential coachee in the role of coach. The areas covered include the complimentary coaching consultation and the welcome packet. In most cases, your initial contact will be a complimentary coaching consultation.

The Complimentary Coaching Consultation

The Complimentary Coaching session is generally a 45-50 minute session. The purpose of the complimentary session is to provide your potential coachee with an opportunity to experience you as a coach, plus for you as the coach to determine the "readiness" of the coachee for coaching. There are three sections to a typical complimentary coaching session. They include:

1. **Introduction of coach and coaching (5-10 minutes):**

- Briefly introduce yourself to the prospective coachee and ask them to do the same.

- Thank them for the opportunity to coach them.

- Take a few moments to explain what coaching is, as well as what it is not.

- Inform the coachee that this is a safe space and you will hold this conversation in confidence.

2. **Complimentary coaching (30 minutes):**

-   Treat this like a real coaching session.

-   During the coaching session develop a next step plan with the coachee and request that they check back with you in two weeks regarding their progress. Ask that they check back with you, even if they do not hire you as their coach. Explain to them that a key component to the coaching process is follow-through and accountability.

3. **Discuss possible next steps (10 minutes):**

-   If the coachee is "ready" for coaching and the relationship between the two of you is positive, talk with the coachee about next steps.

-   Talk with them about the results and benefits of coaching.

-   Share your usual fees, as well as typical next steps to begin a coaching relationship with you.

Remember, some will be ready to hire you right after the complimentary coaching session, some will not. It is not unusual for a prospective coachee to want time to think things through. Give them that time and space. Do not pressure them.

Remind the coachee that whether or not they hire you, you would like to receive a follow-up report from them as to their progress, or lack of progress, in two weeks.

For internal coaching environments, the complimentary coaching session would follow the same process with the following adjustments:

-   A discussion regarding confidentiality of the session and what will and will not be shared with HR, the coachee's manager or others in the organization. NOTE: This also applies to external coaches being hired by a third party to coach internally.

-   Discuss why the coachee is being recommended for or given the coaching opportunity.

-   Fee discussion will likely be non-existent or may include a discussion on department chargebacks and approvals.

The Coaching Welcome Packet

The Welcome Packet is a set of documents that prepare the new coachee for the coaching experience. A sample welcome packet is in the Resources section of this book. The welcome packet includes:

- **A Welcome Letter.** This is an introductory letter that a coach sends to a new coachee that provides the following information:
    - A warm welcome to coaching and a thank you for selecting you as their coach
    - General information about you as the coach, as well as information on the coaching process
    - A coaching agreement
    - Ways for your coachee to prepare for each coaching session. (First Coaching Session Report + Focus Report)
    - The ethics and professional standards you adhere to as a coach
    - Contact information of the coachee

- **The Coaching Agreement.** This is your contract with the coachee. The agreement covers all aspects of the coaching arrangement. It is highly recommended you have an attorney review your contract to ensure it is legally binding and accurate.

- **The Focus Report Form.** This is a form used by the coachee to prepare for the upcoming coaching session. Generally, the form is sent to the coach in advance of each coaching session. Some make this a requirement, while other coaches make it optional. Many coaches have a separate report form for the first coaching session. It often provides the coach with additional information helpful to the coach and the overall coaching process.

For internal coaching environments, the welcome packet would encompass the same general information with the following differences:

- The agreement would be applicable to an internal environment, addressing how information will and will not be shared, and how costs will be expensed.

- Defines how coaching works within the organization's culture and strategy.

SETTING BOUNDARIES

A Boundary is the space you provide between yourself and others—physically, emotionally and mentally.

Healthy boundaries set parameters for the coaching services you will provide and for what you will and will not do, as well as give a clear sense of self. Healthy boundaries define what you need from others, as well as what you will accept from others. They protect the relationships you have with others.

Healthy boundaries allow you to be clear on "who you are" and "what you need." This knowledge promotes a greater sense of peace, joy and confidence in relationships with others, strives for mutual respect and reduces stress. When you set and enforce boundaries in your relationships, it allows you to be accountable for your actions, without taking on the problems of others.

According to the article "Protecting Personal Boundaries" by Laurie Pawlik-Kienlen, personal boundaries are evident and effective when you know who you are, and when you treat yourself and others with respect. When you have healthy boundaries, you have a framework for which to approach situations and people.

To build effective boundaries, you must have clarity around what you need, want, like/dislike, and desire for yourself and your future. The best time to set boundaries is "proactively" before a boundary has been violated versus "reactively" after a boundary has already been violated. Reactive boundary setting can cause a number of issues within a relationship, as expectations will need to be re-established and/or re-negotiated, and negative emotions will likely be heightened, making conflict more likely.

As a coach, when you are building your boundaries, consider the following:

- Be honest with what you want and don't want.
- Determine how you will communicate your boundaries to those you coach.
- Be willing to address and enforce "boundary breaking" with those you coach.

Setting boundaries with those you coach can be done in several different ways. A few options are listed below:

- Discuss boundaries during the initial meeting.
- Include boundaries in your written coaching agreement.
- Spell out expectations in your welcome letter.
- Address boundaries during the coaching process.
- Model boundaries during coaching sessions.

Boundary setting can be difficult, especially for new coaches. The coaching process is often an intimate experience. As coaches, we experience the core of "who" an individual is and support that person's efforts in moving forward. Those we coach share with us their hopes, dreams, goals, disappointments, struggles and challenges. As a result, they may feel a "closeness" to us, which can be advantageous in the coaching process. It can also, in the absence of healthy boundaries, be very dangerous for both the coach and coachee. For this reason, it is important for coaches to set boundaries.

Coaches that have difficulty setting boundaries often:

- Lack healthy self-respect

- Have difficulty with confrontation and conflict management

- Burn out more easily

- Have issues of anger

- Have frustrations and/or feelings of manipulation toward others and/or those they are serving as a coach

- May not be "present-oriented" due to boundary conflicts

- Have issues with "pleasing others"

- Have difficulty being assertive

Setting boundaries is a needed skill for coaches to be effective. In order to be authentic in our communication with those we coach and to not get caught up in their "stuff," coaches must be able to set and enforce effective boundaries. When communicating boundaries it is important to be candid, clear and respectful.

- Be CANDID—share what you are seeing, experiencing, observing.

- Be CLEAR—be specific and concise in your communication.

- Be RESPECTFUL—maintain the self-esteem of others and treat all situations with respect.

As a coach, it is important you have a clear strategy and/or plan for confidently setting boundaries. It is important to be confident and clear on boundaries with those you coach. Likewise, as you get clarity around your boundaries, be clear on when, how and where you will make exceptions. The following are some considerations:

- **Have a Plan for "Boundary Breakers."** Plan in advance how you will address broken boundaries, and how and when you will make exceptions. When a boundary is violated, tactfully discuss expectations going forward. When a boundary requires you to say "no," consider sharing the "why" behind the "no," if appropriate. When a boundary is broken, communicate what will happen next and discuss how to prevent this from happening in the future.

- **Lead by Example.** Have boundaries and use them! Think about those you know who are successful at setting, communicating and enforcing boundaries. Consider how they interact with others and stay true to their boundaries. If you want others to respect your boundaries, make sure you clearly communicate them. Lastly, respect others' boundaries, as you want them to respect your boundaries.

- **Know Your Needs.** Know what you need and desire to be successful. Consider your relationships and your life; define success in your context. Once you know what you need, ask yourself what boundaries you need to put in place to support your success. Lastly, communicate those boundaries to others confidently and without apologies.

- **Proactively Set Boundaries.** Set boundaries "proactively" versus "reactively." Sharing your boundaries in a proactive manner is a better strategy than deciding in the middle of a heated situation that you no longer are going to "take it." Don't put your relationships in jeopardy because you haven't done your homework!

Respect yourself enough to both set and enforce your personal, professional and coaching boundaries. If you cannot enforce your own boundaries, it will be difficult for you to coach others to be the best they can be. For example, as a coach, I have boundaries around my time. There are times I do not coach; I have days set aside for me personally—whether it is to be with my family or rejuvenate myself by following a passion or hobby. How we allow others treat us "trains" them on what we expect in terms of a relationship. When you don't speak up or inform others about your boundaries, you are confirming their behavior is acceptable.

What are the signs and signals indicating a coachee (or anyone) may have issues with boundaries?

- They do not respect your boundaries, as their coach.
- They are constantly stressed.
- They do not know their limits.
- They routinely do not speak up for what they want and need.
- They have difficulty articulating what they want and need.
- They have difficulty with accountability—both in terms of their own accountability and taking on others' accountability issues.
- They habitually sacrifice their needs and wants for the needs and wants of others.

As you work with others in setting boundaries, consider the following techniques to help your coachee develop and/or enhance their ability to set and enforce their boundaries.

Ask the individual to define their needs, wants and goals. Once their goals are defined, have them list the boundaries needed in support of those goals.

- Start by asking the individual what they need to move forward toward their goals.

- Based on that question, ask them to define what boundaries they need to establish to move forward.

- Next, ask the individual to define what support they will need to be successful in implementing and enforcing their boundaries.

- Lastly, ask them to look at their boundaries and consider their ability to assertively enforce these boundaries.

If you notice a pattern of the coachee not speaking up for their boundaries or allowing others to take advantage of them, consider having a discussion about communicating boundaries and self-respect. Look for patterns of deflecting personal accountability or taking on accountability for other people. Ask the individual to define what they are accountable for and get them to define where their accountability begins and ends.

During the coaching process, your coachee will begin to adopt new behaviors and new ways of thinking, and will have new experiences. An important next step is to review and support them in resetting their boundaries. As their coach:

- How are their new behaviors, thinking and experiences impacting how they relate to others?

- How are others interacting with them as they move forward toward their goals?

- Initiate a conversation around boundaries and, when appropriate, share your observations regarding their current boundaries.

Other options for discussion include:

- Discussing the pitfalls of being accountable for other people's actions, situations, etc.

- Discussing the negative impacts of not being accountable for their own actions.

- Discussing the power of setting boundaries and respecting yourself enough to enforce those boundaries.

In summary, I believe setting and enforcing boundaries is one way to ensure your coaching practice thrives. Setting personal and professional boundaries must be done well in order for you to sustain yourself as a coach and to help those you coach move forward effectively.

Chapter Two

The Eight Building Blocks of Coaching

One of my favorite sections in any bookstore is the "How to" section. It's amazing how many "How to" books there are, and they cover an endless array of topics: how to build a deck, fix your car, knit, cook, find your perfect mate, etc.

This section is your coaching "How to." Over the next several pages, you will discover the core competencies and skills of coaching—called the "Building Blocks." These building blocks will provide a framework for your coaching.

1. DEEP LISTENING

All coaching begins with listening!

Don't read any further until you really, REALLY get this. It all begins with listening. Far too often we take listening for granted. How many times has someone tried to help you by offering you a solution without hearing what the problem was? They mean well, but they aren't really helpful. Years ago, I had a medical doctor who would listen to me describe my symptoms for about 13 seconds, and then he would begin backing out the door, prescribing before I had even finished. I quickly learned the art of standing in the doorway.

So, coaching begins with listening—deep listening. The quality of our listening has a direct bearing on the quality of our coaching. You can't draw out the best in another person, or tap into their greatness, if you haven't listened for it.

Listening is one of the greatest gifts you can offer another person. Listening, in and of itself, provides tremendous benefits. Consider the following case study:

Nancy Kline provided an opportunity for every member of a senior management team to listen and be listened to. The result reported was a time savings of 62%. This translated into 2,304 manager hours per year. (*Time to Think, pg. 70.*) That is the equivalent of one full-time person. Think about what could be done with one additional person on a team!

What is listening? Listening is being curious about the other person, conveying that they are valued and important. Listening is about quieting your own mind chatter so you can be fully present with another person. It is about creating a safe space for someone to explore.

It is NOT about giving answers, but EXPLORING possibilities. When you listen deeply you are reflecting back, like a mirror, what you experienced from the person—it is really getting another person.

There is a huge difference between HEARING and LISTENING:

- Hearing is an auditory process. Listening is an intentional process.

- Hearing is done with the ears. Listening involves all of the senses and the total being.

- Hearing includes words, details and information. Listening adds deeper layers.

- Hearing is to know about someone. Listening is knowing someone.

Listening is a skill to be developed.

Good coaches listen so closely the answers almost come out on their own. The ideal listening ratio is to be listening 80% of the time and responding 20% of the time. Someone once told me words comprise about 7% of what we communicate. In other words, most of our communication does not involve words. Coaches know this. That's why coaches listen at multiple levels. Here's a sampling of what a coach is listening for:

- Listen to what the other person is saying, as well as what they are not saying.

- Listen from deep within (gut-level listening).

- Listen to "get" the other person.

- Listen without judgment, criticism or agenda. You are creating a safe place for the person to share.

- Listen without thinking about what you will be saying next.

- Listen for values, frustrations, motivation and needs.

- Listen for the greatness in the person you are coaching.

- Listen for limiting beliefs and false assumptions. What does this person really believe the outcome or future will be?

- Listen for shoulds, oughts and musts. They are frequent indicators of obligation and guilt versus what the person really wants.

- Listen for the obvious. What is the other person not seeing or not aware of?

- Listen for the tone, pace, volume, inflection and frequently used words. Also, notice when these change.

- Listen for the larger context.

- Listen attentively to the end of the statements. Remember the old faucets with well water? You needed to let them run awhile before you got the good water. The best words often flow out last as well!

- Listen to your reactions as you listen.

To be able to listen at multiple levels, a coach must quiet their mind of any mind chatter or internal conversations. They must create a physical environment that promotes deep listening, by attending to the space and pace of life and by managing their schedule and calendar. Coaches grow to be comfortable with silence—resisting the urge to fill the space. As a new coach, I recall a seasoned coach saying deep listening is similar to standing in a pool. In order to see the bottom clearly, you must be still—absolutely still.

Pause for a moment and consider your own potential barriers to deep listening. What are some steps you can take to address these challenges?

Here are some exercises to improve your listening:

- **Mute the TV.** Since most of what is communicated is non-verbal, why not mute the TV and have some fun trying to guess what's being communicated? To really test this ability, tape the TV show, watch it with the sound muted, and then watch it again with the sound playing.

- **Mirroring.** Pair up with a partner, with each person taking a turn to talk and to listen. When you're the listener, do your best to listen as if you were a mirror. Reflect back what you heard. Then ask: Did I get that right? Did I hear you correctly?

- **Record a conversation.** With the permission of the other person, record a conversation in which you intentionally attempted to listen deeply. Right after the conversation, write down what your deep listening revealed. Then, go back and listen to the recording of the conversation. What more did you hear? What had you missed?

- **Practice selective listening.** Decide for the next week that you are going to be selective in your listening and really listen for one specific element. For example, you might choose to identify the values you hear underneath people's words. Or you might listen only for signs of frustration, or for signs of greatness. Over the course of the week, pay attention to that one select area, training yourself to listen for this one item. Notice when you hear the item clearly—what circumstances made that possible in you and around you? What was going on in the times when it was challenging to hear the item?

Remember, great listeners hear with their:

- **Ears.** They listen to the spoken words, as well as tone, pace, pitch and inflection. They listen for the essence of what is being said.

- **Eyes.** Most of our communication is non-verbal. Great listeners notice body language of the one speaking.

- **Full body and being.** Gifted listeners notice how they are receiving the message. They pay attention to what is happening inside of them as they listen.

2. POWERFUL QUESTIONS

On one of my recent travels to deliver a coach training program, I heard a statement on the radio that stopped me cold. History changed when a single question changed—when we stopped asking, "How do we get to the water?" and started asking, "How do we get the water to us?" What a radical shift for us as human beings! Consider how this relates to us as leaders and individuals in organizations. How would our teams and organizations change if we were to change our questions?

For example, here are some of the questions you might be asking now:

1. How do we get our customers to come to us?
2. How much longer can we afford this?
3. How do we get our employees to buy into this?

Boards and leaders literally spend hours on question #1, but I think that if the question changed, different outcomes could be produced. What if you asked, "How can we get to our customers?" or "How can we have a positive impact on our customers?"

Question #2 suggests scarcity thinking—focusing on what's lacking instead of what's abundant. What if you ask, "What more can we do with the resources we have?" or "How can we develop the people we have so they can make a bigger contribution and everyone wins?"

In question #3, it sounds like you are trying to cajole or even manipulate people into doing something they don't really want to do. What if you ask, "What can we do to make the greatest impact and how can we garner support? People are happy to invest time, energy and resources when it impacts the vision and others positively.

I invite you to listen for the questions you and your team and/or organization are asking. Are they limiting, like our examples above, or are they powerful? And what's the difference?

One of a coach's greatest tools is powerful questions. Powerful questions are usually open-ended, leaving room for contemplation and reflection, instead of being limited to yes or no or specific choices. Powerful questions promote the exploration of new possibilities and stimulate creativity. They place the individual or group in a place of responsibility. They empower individuals and groups to consider what is right for them.

Powerful questions open up possibilities beyond the reality that's in front of us today, stretching us into the territory of our visions to ask, "What is the opportunity for us in this situation?"

Limiting questions, on the other hand, might not be questions at all. They may only be thinly masking a statement of blame, obligation or guilt; for example, "Why did you do it that way?"

Here are a few powerful questions for consideration:

- How could you make better use of your personal strengths?
- How could you make better use of the strengths of your team and/or organization?
- What kind of leader would you be if you were driven by passion?
- Which of your roles could someone else be doing, and probably better than you?
- What's the worst thing that could happen if you did less?

What makes a question powerful? Powerful questions are:

- **Directly connected to deep listening.** Early on in my coaching career I believed there was only one "right" question. I would equip myself with a long list of questions I could scan while coaching. What I quickly discovered was the most powerful questions were created in the moment and the power of the question was directly related to my ability to listen deeply.

- **Brief.** They get right to the point. Resist adding an explanation or another question, instead of just waiting for the person to respond.

- **Free of any hidden agenda.** They are not leading or suggestive. In the coaching profession we refer to leading questions as "que-ggestions." Powerful questions help the person or group being coached to move further along the path of discovery.

- **Usually open-ended, promoting further conversation.** For the most part, yes/no questions usually result in a yes/no response, which force an end to the conversation and enable either/or thinking. Powerful questions promote both/and thinking, opening the coachee to a fuller range of possibilities.

- **Clarifying.** They help clarify and slow down automatic responses and thinking. My clients have told me time and time again they appreciate how coaching creates the opportunity for them to step aside—push the pause button—and discern what they really want.

- **Perspective-shifting.** Powerful questions invite the coachee to walk across to the other side of the room and look at the same thing from a different angle or perspective.

- **Benefits the one we are coaching.** Remember that the coach is not the expert and does not have to figure anything out or come up with solutions. Therefore, our questions must be designed to help the coachee discover and develop their own perspective and wisdom about the situation.

Types of powerful questions

Questions that help the person gain perspective and understanding:

- What's the truth about this situation?
- Who do you remind yourself of?
- What keeps you up at night?
- Is there anything else that would be important for me to know?

Questions that evoke discovery:

- What do you really, really want?
- What's perfect about this?
- What is the silver lining in this?
- What additional information do you need?
- How much is this costing you?
- Who can help you with this?

Questions that promote clarity and learning:

- What if things are as bad as you say they are?
- Where are you sabotaging yourself?
- What's the cost of not changing?
- What's next?
- What's past this issue?

Questions that call for action:

- What's possible today?
- How soon can you resolve this?
- Who do you know that's going through this?
- What does success look like?
- What's the first step? When will you take this step?

> "People remember ... things they discover, learn and experience themselves. If you want someone to digest and remember something...ask him a question."
> ~ Dorothy Leeds, Smart Questions

At the beginning of this section on powerful questions, you read that history changed when a single question changed. Questions are a powerful tool at our disposal. A powerful question, created out of deep listening, can change everything. Change the questions, change your organization.

Top 10 Questions

1. On a scale of 1 to 10, how would you rate...?
2. What's the payoff of not taking action?
3. What's the truth about this situation?
4. What's your vision?
5. What's past this?

at keeps getting in the way?

aat's the simplest solution?

ho can help you with this?

9. What do you think about when you're lost in thought?

10. What do you really, REALLY want?

Below are exercises, strategies and examples to further develop your understanding and use of powerful questions:

- **Scenario #1:** Your leadership team has been unable to take action on something decided months ago. Your team seems stuck on this issue. What powerful questions could you ask?

- **Scenario #2:** You are designing a new service offering and are looking for a specific response from key stakeholders. What powerful questions could you ask?

- **Scenario #3:** You are meeting with a team who is struggling to work together effectively. The team members have a fairly healthy relationship with each other but are stuck on this one issue. Several team members are blaming each other. What powerful questions could you ask this team?

A common complaint we hear from leaders relates to engagement and input from team members. They often ask, "How do we get people to share their ideas and comments at our meetings? We send out the agenda ahead of time and no one seems prepared to discuss things."

A simple change to using questions in the agenda format can often jumpstart the discussion. Instead of creating an agenda with topics to discuss, develop a couple of questions from your original agenda to start people thinking. For example,

Original agenda:

1. Financial Update

2. Leadership Team Report

3.   Team Metrics Update

4.   Other

Revised agenda with questions:

1.   What are some ways to generate additional revenue during our slow summer months?

2.   We need to develop a new hiring and retention strategy. Who has some thoughts to share on this topic?

3.   We have a trend over the last three months of not achieving our customer satisfaction metric. What is our next step?

4.   What other items should we be addressing today?

3. ARTFUL LANGUAGE

Many of us grew up hearing the statement "sticks and stones may break my bones, but words can never harm me." Nothing could be further from the truth!

Our words matter! Our language can provide a platform that motivates someone forward to peak performance, the perfect career or becoming a better leader. At the same time, our language can reinforce doubts and limiting beliefs—dashing hopes and dreams. Think of language like a scalpel; in the hands of the skilful and altruistic, it can be invaluable, while in the hand of the reckless or malicious, it can have devastating effects. Language is like the paintbrush in a coach's hand; it is the playground for our meaningful work.

Let's check out four pieces of equipment on the coach's playground:

*   Our actual words.

*   Matching of words.

*   Distinctions.

*   Acknowledgement.

Our Actual Words

Ask yourself—how are my chosen words resonating with the other person? In coaching, we often refer to this as how something "lands." Are my actual words fostering a safe and inviting environment that encourages the other person to go deeper below the surface to the core issues? Or, is the other person so busy dodging and ducking the zingers you're hurling at them they can only say "ouch!"

In our day-to-day conversations, words often contain assumptions, presuppositions, judgments, manipulation and suggestions. In coaching conversations, we intentionally choose words that are neutral, non-manipulative and free of any agenda. Our tone of voice is equally important. The same word with a different tone can be received entirely differently.

The Matching of Words and Language

Coaches notice the words and phrases of the other person. When appropriate, a coach will match their words and phrases with the person they are coaching and introduce new words or phrases. Coaches also pay attention to the pace and pattern of the other person's language. For example, when asked a question, introverts tend to process first and then talk, while extroverts tend to process by talking to arrive at an answer. The seasoned coach will sometimes match the other person to convey a feeling of acceptance; other times he or she will intentionally change up the pace and pattern to get the coachee's attention and make a point.

The coach is also listening for words that help the other person learn, describe their values and define their reality. These can be very useful in facilitating a shift. Often these are popular words or phrases from current or past culture. They can include TV, movies, music, metaphors, stories and quotes.

Examples of metaphors:

- The fruit doesn't fall far from the tree.
- Breaking the glass ceiling.
- Swimming in a sea of choices.
- Drinking from a fire-hose.
- Pulling yourself up by your bootstraps.
- It sounds like you're on a see-saw.
- It doesn't work to leap a 20-foot chasm in two 10-foot jumps. (American proverb)

Examples of stories:

- The "Emperor's New Clothes" and the importance of truth-telling.

- Forrest Gump's "Life is like a box of chocolates."

- Humpty-Dumpty's lesson that some things in life can never be put back together again.

Examples of quotes:

- "And the day came when the risk to remain tight in a bud was more painful than the risk it took to blossom." —Anais Nin

- "It is a terrible thing to look over your shoulder when leading and find no one there." —Franklin Delano Roosevelt

- "Most leaders don't need to learn what to do. They need to learn what to stop." —Peter Drucker

Examples from popular media culture include:

- The song "Don't Worry, Be Happy."

- "You're fired!" from Donald Trump's TV show *The Apprentice*.

- The TV show *Survivor* and the phrase "getting voted off the island."

- A place "where everybody knows your name," as revered in the theme song of the long-running TV show *Cheers*.

Distinctions

Distinctions are two words or phrases that are close in meaning, yet convey subtle differences. Those subtle differences create a new awareness that is instrumental in propelling the individual forward.

Consider the following distinction and the subtle, yet huge, shift it creates—definition by obstacles versus definition by opportunities:

- To define yourself by obstacles means you are defining who you are and the decisions you make based on the challenges you are facing. A life defined by obstacles is reactive. It is moving away from someone or something.

- To define yourself by opportunities means you define who you are and base your decisions on your opportunities. It's not that you're ignoring the obstacles, you've just decided to keep your sights on the bigger picture—your vision. It is moving toward someone or something and is usually proactive.

Additional distinctions:

- Perfection versus excellence.

- Adding more versus adding value.

- Living by default versus living by design.

- Working hard versus producing results.

- Either/or versus both/and.

- Prioritizing what's on your schedule versus scheduling your priorities.

- Doing powerfully effective things versus being powerfully effective.

- Planning versus preparing.

Distinctions are a much more subtle version of the "shifts" that often occur when a coachee takes the awareness created in the coaching session and puts it into action. Below are five shifts coaches might want to consider to move forward effectively as a coach:

- From diagnosing to developing

- From doing to empowering

- From telling to exploring

- From mindlessness to mindfulness

- From excellence to effectiveness

Acknowledgment

Most people, when asked to create a list of their weaknesses and also a list of their strengths, find it easier to list their weaknesses. Why? Many people assume if I can just fix my weaknesses or if I could only correct what's wrong with me, eventually I will be great!

Consider the following: The average person, on any given day, has between 12,000 to 50,000 thoughts. By the age of eight, most of those thoughts are negative thoughts (e.g., I'm not good enough. I can't do it. What's wrong with me?). Your organization and, in fact, the entire world is made up of people who already speak to themselves with judgment and disapproval.

Acknowledgment creates an environment of acceptance and safety. When people feel safe and accepted, they are more likely to be curious and explore new things.

I mentioned Ben Zander earlier; he understands the importance of acknowledgment. When he uses his "A" approach in class, he is not only focusing on the person his students will become but he is also acknowledging the greatness within his students and is inviting them to live into that greatness.

> "We are not expected to be who we are not. We are expected to be who we are."
> — Albert L. Winseman, et al, *Living Your Strengths*

Effective organizations will be about giving an "A"—genuinely tapping into people's greatness. Imagine if organizations were known for giving "A's," instead of judgment. Or, if the focus of organizations shifted from what they are not to who they are, as well as who they are becoming, what shifts would occur? How different would organizations be if leaders regularly focused on acknowledging the strengths of employees? How different would you or your organization be if you approached life from Ben Zander's perspective? What shifts would occur in you, your family and your sphere of influence?

Remember Nancy Kline and her book *Time to Think* (pages 62-64)? We read about how society teaches us to be positive is to be naïve and vulnerable, whereas to be critical is to be informed, buttressed and sophisticated. Many people are taught that to be appreciated is a slippery slope towards gross immodesty. It's as if, when you hear something nice about yourself and don't reject it instantly, you will, presto, turn into an out-of-control egomaniac. This is ridiculous.

Actually, change takes place best in a large context of genuine praise, Kline asserts. Appreciation (what we are calling acknowledgment) is important not because it feels good or is nice, but because it helps people think for themselves on the cutting edge of an issue. We should aim for a 5:1 ratio of appreciation to criticism. Being appreciated increases your intelligence and helps you think better.

4. ACTION AND ACCOUNTABILITY

At a training program where I began exploring action and accountability, a participant at the coach training event declared, "Finally, the good stuff!" When asked what he meant he said that everything we had discussed up until now, while helpful information, didn't really matter unless action happened. In many respects, he was right. One of the primary reasons a person or a group decides to work with a coach is that they want to take action and reach their goals.

Action and forward progress are indeed the good stuff. There are three components to action and accountability:

1. Brainstorming

2. Designing the action

3. Follow through

It's really tempting at this point in the coaching process to jump right in and design an action plan. I want you to resist that urge and instead take a few more moments to brainstorm. Why am I suggesting this? Our coachee's tendency is going to be to take similar action steps as before, if not the same exact actions. The trouble is those same action steps are going to generate the same outcomes. The reason this person or group is in coaching is to get different results!

> Nothing changes, if nothing changes.

Brainstorming

Brainstorming helps someone see the same thing differently. Brainstorming enables the individual to discover for themselves different perspectives and possibilities. This involves distinguishing between fact, perception and interpretation, as well as gaining clarity and defining success.

I want those I coach to have those kinds of epiphanies when we brainstorm together before creating an action plan. I usually start by asking them to identify a next step—what they would usually do next. Then, I ask them to set that action aside for the moment and come up with several other possible actions. Most laugh at this request. Many are speechless. I re-state my request and give them some prompts, such as:

• What's the most outrageous step you could take?

• What's the simplest next step?

• Who could help you generate more ideas for next steps?

• What possibilities have you repeatedly dismissed?

Years ago I coached a leader about casting the vision for his organization. His usual method of vision-casting was to present a compelling vision at the beginning of each new year. Upon inquiry he acknowledged this method stirred people for a couple of days but produced no real progress. I then asked him to set that action step aside and requested over the next two weeks that he identify 50 other ways to cast vision. He repeatedly stated he didn't know any others, and I repeatedly requested he come up with his list.

Two weeks later he came back with a list of 50 ways to catch the vision. Here's how he did it: The day after our previous coaching session, he went to his leadership team and kiddingly told the team about the outrageous request his coach had made of him—50 ways to cast the vision. One of his leadership team members jokingly referred to the rock song "50 Ways to Leave Your Lover" and another team member laughingly said we could put together a song called "50 Ways to Cast Our Vision" and present it to our employees at our annual sales meeting. In the following moments, with the help of his leadership team, he started considering 50 other ways to cast vision. Now he was ready to design the action plan!

Designing the Action

Within the context of brainstorming, a plan begins to emerge. The plan includes next steps that are attainable, measurable, specific and have target dates. In most cases the plan addresses both what you need to do and who you need to become in order to reach your goal. Commitment then usually comes naturally and effortlessly.

Techniques useful for designing the action include:

- **Baby steps.** Sometimes people are immobilized with all that needs to happen. Breaking the action steps into smaller steps can help them begin taking action.

- **Backward planning.** Begin at the end (the goal) and then move backward and develop steps to get to the goal.

- **Acknowledging.** Recognizing what has been accomplished.

- **Creating structure.** Identifying what and who will keep the client focused on the task at hand.

- **Strategizing.** Considering what might derail progress and design action steps in advance.

- **Anchoring.** Regularly reminding the person or group of the importance of what they are doing and where they are in the plan.

- **"Blitz Days."** Helping them carve out solid blocks of time to tackle everything that is getting in the way or needs to be done to stay on task.

- **Identify daily action.** These help create daily movement and momentum.

Sometimes formulas can be helpful. Consider the G.R.O.W. Model:

G	Goal	What's the goal?
R	(Current) Reality	How are we doing?
O	Opportunities	What are our current opportunities?
W	What	What's the next step?

Follow Through

In an ongoing coaching relationship, you are checking in regarding ongoing progress and course corrections. In most cases, I coach people twice a month—that's two times every month for us to follow through. I usually begin each coaching session with questions like these:

- What's happened since the last time we met?
- What didn't happen that you really intended to happen?
- What got in the way? What were the challenges?
- What will you report back to me the next time we meet, regarding this action?
- What do you want to focus on today?

Notice that the accountability is palatable as we define completion. There is no judgment or shame involved. There is no guilt or manipulation. This ongoing accountability is a natural part of the coaching relationship. A leader once stated that accountability is really about "goaltending."

5. THE COACHING RELATIONSHIP

In real estate, the three most important things are: location, location and location. It can also be stated that, in coaching, the three most important things are: relating, relating and relating. The coaching relationship is the vehicle of change and transformation.

One way to view the coaching relationship is as a dance. Let's use the example of the great dance couple Fred Astaire and Ginger Rogers to describe the dance of the coaching relationship. Consider Fred Astaire as the coachee and Ginger Rogers the coach. Notice that Ginger did everything Fred did (only backwards and in high heels!) but that she takes her lead from Fred.

Let's stay with the dance of coaching to further understand the unique and skillful way in which a coach relates. Fred and Ginger developed a safety and trust that let them draw close to each other. A level of intimacy was present, yet never violated. This allowed them to really "get" each other and almost anticipate each other's moves. Coaches are able to be totally spontaneous, while also being fully present and in the moment. This total spontaneity involves a knowing beyond what is typically, or rationally, known and observed. It's similar to the athlete who can anticipate where the ball will be thrown, before it's thrown.

New coaches often ask, "How do you further develop coaching presence—your own deeper level of knowing?" There are no shortcuts to develop a deeper level of knowing. It all begins with deep listening. Practice listening, and then practice again and again. Develop and use powerful questions, and make artful choices with your language. Here are some additional tools that have helped others:

- **Note-taking.** The act of writing helps many go deeper. Jot down what you're noticing in the coaching session. Remember, deep listening uses the eyes, as well as the ears. The challenge of note-taking is to take notes in such as way it enhances rather than interferes with your deep listening.

- **Self-care.** It's hard to go deeper when you're barely managing life on the surface. Like they tell us on airplanes—place the mask on yourself first and then your children. Similarly, take care of yourself first before you attempt to assist others.

- **Review your coaching.** Record a coaching session and then review it. Then take it one step further and ask your mentor-coach to review it and give you feedback, specifically about your coaching presence.

- **Quiet your mind.** Intentionally quiet yourself before and after a coaching session. Show up with a clean frame of reference and a quiet mind. Then spend time reflecting after the session on what worked and what you might do differently the next time you coach.

- **Risk.** Share your hunches, inklings or gut feelings. Preface your hunch by saying something like "I'd like to go out on a skinny branch for a moment with you. I could be completely wrong, but here's what I'm wondering (or noticing)…"

- **Listen from the heart versus the head (or vice versa).** Be intentional in shifting from intellect to intuition. Request that the person you are coaching also get out of their head and listen from the heart. Ask them "What are you feeling in your body right now? What might your body be trying to tell you?"

Let's go back to Fred and Ginger for another unique component of the coaching relationship. Notice that Fred and Ginger aren't trying to correct or judge each other's steps while they dance. There is a mutual respect for the other's level of skills and competence. They each have their unique experience, strength and gifts. And the way they relate to each other brings out the best in the other. On the dance floor they are tapped into each other's strengths.

In your day-to-day work and personal life, practice intentionally listening and looking for greatness. At first you'll probably notice how much easier it is to diagnose and how frequently you miss the opportunities to develop others. Be kind to yourself—most of today's leaders, paid and unpaid, have been formally and informally trained to diagnose problems, not necessarily to develop others. Over time you'll begin to notice those "development" moments.

Next, begin to tell others what you notice about their strengths and gifts. They may dismiss it or disqualify it. Keep telling them anyway, because what's important is the shift you're making in how you relate to them—as a partner in their success. Eventually, like Fred and Ginger, you'll be tapping into the strengths of others with ease and grace. And you'll also notice your new way of relating will be an attractive magnet for drawing people to you and your team or organization.

A positive coaching relationship will increase your coachee's likelihood of success. Since they relate well to you, they are more likely to explore further and take bigger steps, plus they will stick with their plan of action longer.

6. THE COACHING AGREEMENT

As leaders, we often find ourselves saying, "If you need something from me, please tell me. If I don't know what you need or want, I can only guess at what you need and want. I am not a mind reader."

The same is true of coaches—we aren't mind readers—that's why we have a coaching agreement. A coaching agreement is a way to define the requirements and process behind the coaching relationship. The coaching agreement takes most of the guesswork out of coaching and makes it possible for the coach to follow the coachee—not the other way around.

While newer coaches see the coaching agreement as a once-and-done process, masterful coaches understand the ongoing nature of the coaching agreement. There are three parts to the coaching agreement:

- The initial agreement

- The ongoing agreement

- The evaluation process

The initial coaching agreement defines the terms of the coaching relationship in writing. For example, the initial coaching agreement includes: fees, schedule, responsibilities, and expectations of the coach and coachee. If you are an internal coach we still recommend you have a coaching agreement that outlines expectations. The coaching agreement articulates what coaching is and isn't, and clarifies the needs of the coachee and why they want to work with a coach.

I usually have a conversation with the coachee to ask them questions like "What do you want to be able to say three months from now that you cannot say today?" This helps both the coach and coachee gain clarity about the desired outcome.

The ongoing coaching agreement includes:

- Helping the coachee clarify what they want to focus on in each particular coaching session, as well as what they want to take away.

- Further clarifying and exploring what the coachee is taking away from the coaching session.

- Holding side-by-side the initial desired outcomes and goals that brought them to coaching and the current focus/take-away. Because coaching is focused on discovery and not outcomes, new insights and perspectives need to be continually integrated into the coaching agreement.

The third component of the coaching agreement is the evaluation process. This frequently includes course corrections, or may also involve a dramatic shift in the overall desired outcome. Questions include:

- How are we doing?

- Based on our coaching to date, what's your ongoing, developing vision?

- On a scale of 1-10, rate the overall progress you've made. What is needed to take it up several levels?

- What more do I need to know about you, your learning preferences, or background to accelerate your progress/performance?

- Where is self-sabotage showing up?

- What additional supports are needed?

- What will you report back to me the next time we meet?

A frequent mistake new coaches make is in moving through the coaching agreement quickly—in as little as two to five minutes. The clearer the coachee and coach are with the agreement, the better the outcome. It's not unusual to spend the bulk of a coaching session on this area—15-20 minutes. Here are questions and statements that help coachees and their coaches fine-tune the coaching agreement and evaluate the coaching process:

- Tell me more. Because people are so busy, they rarely have time to think and talk. It's extremely beneficial to intentionally provide space for people to say more. Time and time again we hear coachees extol the benefits of "getting things out."

- What is the one thing I need to hear in order to best coach you? This helps the coachee get laser-focused and selective about sharing only what's absolutely critical to their overall progress.

- Taking into account all that's on your plate right now, is this topic/issue the most important one (and if not, what is)? Similarly, this question helps the coachee hone in on the topics and issues that will contribute the most to their overall success and satisfaction.

This coaching scenario will help you to further understand the coaching agreement:

Steve is the founder and senior leader of a rapidly growing company. He currently has 22 full-time employees on his team. He frequently describes his team as a family. It's not unusual for Steve to "go the extra mile" and bend the rules for individual members of his team, because he considers them to be his family. He finds it difficult to reprimand them and to implement performance plans, let alone even consider firing anyone, because he really views his staff as family and is concerned with their well-being.

Steve's vision is to grow into a global organization. He believes he can do this within the next three to five years. In addition to implementing this global vision, he would also like to spend less time at work and enjoy life more. His big dream is to take six weeks off next summer and tour Europe with his family, and let his leadership team run the company in his absence.

Steve has created a strategic plan and action steps to move towards his goal. He's making moderate progress. He is becoming very aware that his current leadership team is slowing things down. He is also frustrated his "company family" doesn't share the enthusiasm for his vision. Steve hired a coach to help him implement his global plan, with a special emphasis on how he can empower and equip the leadership team to lead the implementation of the plan.

During a recent coaching session, Steve expressed frustration about his vision and his "company family," and then made the following statement about himself: "Maybe I'm the one that's holding back this vision. It feels like all the pieces are there, but maybe there's something that needs to change about me."

In your words, describe the focus of this coaching relationship (as may have been determined in the initial coaching agreement).

What are Steve's new discoveries? What other new discoveries do you see ahead for Steve?

In what ways will these new discoveries impact the coaching agreement?

In what ways will the coaching agreement remain the same?

After hearing Steve state, "Maybe I'm the one that's holding us back," how would you coach Steve?

7. CREATING NEW AWARENESS

Brainstorming is an excellent way to explore new ways of doing things. Creating awareness takes it one step further and explores new ways of being, as well as doing. It's like working the plates deep within the earth, resulting in major shifts and changes.

Here are some examples of creating awareness:

- Consider this statement from one leader I coached: "I'm an introvert and everyone knows that introverts aren't good leaders." No amount of doing would result in any lasting change. This individual needed to go down deep and create a new awareness of his strengths.

- Consider the leadership team that fizzled out partway through a visioning process. The consultant tried everything to get them moving and then finally inquired what was happening. After what seemed like an eternity of silence, one of the key leaders finally responded that they had gotten to this point on two previous occasions within the past five years and, in each instance, their leader had moved on before the projects were completed. No sooner had the words been spoken when the leadership team had a major "a-ha." They embraced their new awareness and began moving forward.

- Consider the awareness that launched my career as a full-time coach. As a part-time coach, my business growth was slowed by the belief that "he is just a pastor" and no one would hire a pastor as their coach. When my coach helped me verbalize this limiting belief, it created an awareness of the truth that my ideal clients will seek me out and hire me precisely because I am a pastor.

Creating new awareness is like raising the blinds and letting in the light of additional information, perspective and intention. New awareness is fostered when curiosity is encouraged. When you use clarifying questions to dig deeper, beliefs and assumptions can be articulated and verified. Awareness is created when you help those you coach intentionally consider a different perspective and be open to other ways of viewing and interpreting the same situation.

Facilitating new awareness happens when the following occurs:

- **Contextual listening.** The coach considers and explores the various contexts of the person being coached (e.g., the bigger picture, the total person, previous experiences, and the values of the person).

- **Missing pieces.** The coach helps individuals and groups see and say what they can't quite see or say. Because the coach is listening on multiple levels, the coach hears underlying values, motivation, greatness, frustration, etc. Simply being a mirror and holding up for the other what we're observing creates new awareness.

- **Drilling down.** Similar to the layers of an onion, the coaching process peels away the layers and gets to the core issues.

- **Listening for clues.** A coachee is always offering clues about themselves. Here are some powerful questions that will uncover important clues:
    - What kind of problems and crises do you keep attracting?
    - What do you keep doing that limits your success?
    - What thoughts are repeatedly playing in your head?

> "The range of what we think and do is limited by what we fail to notice. And because we fail to notice that we fail to notice, there is little we can do to change; until we notice how failing to notice shapes our thoughts and deed."
> – R.D. Lang

Limiting Beliefs and False Assumptions

One of the most powerful ways of creating awareness in a coaching relationship is to help the coachee identify and transform their limiting beliefs and false assumptions.

Use the following list to see if you recognize some of your own:

- I have to have all the answers.
- I have no choice.
- I have no power.
- I cannot lead.
- Change is always difficult.
- It isn't possible.
- What doesn't kill you makes you stronger.
- Peace is always better than honesty.

List three of your limiting beliefs:

1. _____

2. _____

3. _____

List three of your false assumptions:

1. _____

2. _____

3. _____

Limiting beliefs and false assumptions can be very simple, yet very harmful. In her book *Time to Think*, Nancy Kline offers a simple yet profound method of dealing with limiting beliefs and false assumptions. One of her tips is to help your coachee articulate the "positive opposite" of their limiting belief or false assumption. This is often a difficult task for an individual or team to do, but press them to articulate the positive opposite of their bedrock assumption. Once articulated, ask them to write it down, brainstorm ways to act on it, and then support them as they put it into action.

8. DIRECT COMMUNICATION

If you spend time with a seasoned coach, you will notice the masterful way that they communicate. For example, you will almost never hear a masterful coach ramble. Most seasoned coaches are clear, concise and laser-like with their words, offering one question or statement at a time.

Another characteristic is their comfort with silence. There is no attempt to idly fill space; rather, an appropriate use of silence and pauses is demonstrated. And coaches tell the truth. They don't hold back on whatever needs to be said, even if it isn't always the nicest thing to hear or the most comfortable thing to say.

Seasoned coaches are direct in their communication, using language that will have the greatest positive impact on the person being coached. Four of the most important direct communication techniques are:

- Interrupting
- Advising

- Directing
- Messaging

Interrupting

Most of us have experienced interruptions as distracting or annoying, but effective interrupting is truly an art. As a coaching skill, masterful interrupting holds great benefit for the coachee, bringing them back on task, or helping them to "bottom-line" (get to the point).

Coaches interrupt within an environment of trust and intimacy, one in which the coachee trusts the skill of the coach and knows the coach has their best interest in mind. Interrupting can stem from deep listening, as a means of getting at something even deeper that needs to be said. Interrupting is a platform from which to catapult the coachee forward.

During my initial coaching sessions with new coachees, part of the initial agreement is for them to give me permission to interrupt them, when appropriate. Having this conversation on the front-end of the coaching experience helps the coachee expect the interruptions and see them in a positive light.

Here are several ways to interrupt someone while coaching:

- Say their name and ask for permission; e.g., "(Name), may I interrupt you?"
- Break in with "Let's push the pause button for a moment," or "I'd like to step in for a moment."
- Bottom-line it for them, e.g.; "(Name), here's what I'm hearing..."

Advising

One of the myths of coaching is that coaches never give advice. That's a myth? Let me explain. First and foremost, the coach wants to tap into the expertise of the one they are coaching. There are also times when the coach has expertise and experiences that can have a positive impact on the forward progress of the coachee. During a workshop at an International Coach Federation conference, the presenter stated that #7 on the top 10 list of what people want in a coach is advice. The qualifiers are they want advice from their coach *when appropriate* and *when asked for*.

The problem with giving advice is that most people offer advice in ways that are disempowering of others. They need to unlearn how to give *advice* and then re-learn how to *advise*. We suggest newer coaches completely refrain from offering advice, at least for a time. Once they have learned how to effectively coach without giving advice, they can begin incorporating advising into their coaching when appropriate and when asked for.

Consider the following tips when advising:

- Listen deeply. Hear all the person has to say.
- Don't offer advice until you have thought through how the advice may be misheard.
- Don't give advice until you have heard all the facts.
- Don't forget it's ONLY ADVICE; it's not a cure for global warming.
- Phrasing examples:
    - Here's what I've seen work. Tell me if it sounds like it's worth experimenting with.
    - That's a tough one. Here's what I advised another person and this is what happened.

Directing

Directing is a technique for re-focusing or steering the person or group back toward their goals. This is useful for the coachee who frequently goes off on tangents or easily loses sight of the big picture.

Examples of directing:

- Hold that thought and let's talk about...
- For the past several weeks we've been focusing on ABC. Is it time to move on to XYZ?
- Congratulations. What should we focus on now?

Messaging

Messaging is a "truth" that, if heard, will help the other person to understand and act more quickly. It is a "blending" of acknowledging and tapping into the person's greatness.

Examples of messaging include:

- Tell them who they are. "You are someone who is… "

- Endorse what they have accomplished. "Wow. Look what you've accomplished. Congratulations."

- Tell them what's next. "You probably need to start focusing on ABC, since you've moved past XYZ."

- Tell them what you want for them. "What I want for you is…"

Chapter Three

Common Coaching Scenarios in Business and Corporate Coaching

This chapter is designed to provide you with a basic understanding of several common coaching situations experienced as a coach in a variety of settings. While the coaching of each person or group is unique, there are often common themes and approaches.

A Few General Comments about This Resource Material

- The purpose of this material is not to pigeonhole coachees or to put them in a "one-size-fits-all" category. The purpose is to provide useful tools and insights for coaching those in various settings.

- This material is intended to be a resource guide to help identify and understand the common needs and outcomes of those you may encounter in your coaching.

The eight common coaching scenarios we will address include:

1. Coaching a Husband and Wife
2. Coaching for Healthy Living
3. Coaching the CEO and Executive
4. Coaching the Job Transition
5. Coaching Promotions
6. Coaching Behavior that Sabotages
7. Coaching the Non-Profit Leader
8. Coaching for Leadership Development

Scenario #1: Husband and Wife – Adult Children Living at Home

Sue and Clark have been married for 25 years. They have two adult children, John (24 years old) and Karen (23 years old). When John and Karen graduated from high school and went to college, the transition for Sue and Clark went smoothly. Summers at home, along with school breaks throughout the year, were a happy time for all four adults in this family.

Both John and Karen have now graduated from college and both are now living at home with their parents, Sue and Clark. John has been unable to secure a job in his field and is currently working at McDonald's. Karen has been fortunate to be hired in her field, but the pay is very low. She is currently unable to support herself financially. Both John and Karen are very frustrated with having to live at home.

Sue and Clark want to be supportive and helpful to their children. While they recognize that many college graduates are ending up in this same situation, they are also feeling the stress of having four adults living together in the same house. Everyone is doing their best to make things work and the stress levels are high.

Sue and Clark have noticed that they have been arguing a lot more lately. They are also concerned that years from now their children will look back on this time of their lives and resent their parents. Sue and Clark have hired a life coach to help them work things out now and to also address their long range concerns.

What are the key issues Sue and Clark are addressing?

- One key issue would be helping this couple gain greater clarity about what the real issue is, as well as identifying their common goal.

- It would also be important to explore the expectations that each family member brings to this scenario.

- Involving the adult children in this conversation would be necessary.

What requests would you make of them individually? As a couple?

- I would request that, as a couple, that they intentionally involve the adult children in this conversation.

- In addition, I would also request that individually, and as a couple, that Sue and Clark identify their vision for their marriage and their family.

How would you coach Sue and Clark?

- I would want to offer both individual and couples coaching.

- As stated above, I would also recommend that the entire family be involved in the coaching process.

- One strategy would be: what could we do right now, this week? What would be the simplest step?

What, if any, tools and resources would you use with them?

- I would have each person complete the Wheel of Life exercise. After Sue and Clark had identified the eight key areas of their relationship, I would have them complete the wheel individually and then share their results with each other. This exercise would serve to help them identify key coaching areas.

Scenario #2: Brad — 49-Year-Old Brad Wants to Lose Weight and Become Healthier

Brad is 49 years old and has recently decided that he wants to lose weight and become much healthier. During his 20s and 30s, he was very active playing sports and weight training. Several years ago, when he received a major promotion at work, he became very inactive. The result is that he has gained 75 pounds and suffers from severe headaches and backaches.

Several months ago, his doctor said that the only thing wrong with Brad was his weight and that now was the time for him to start being physically active, before any major health issues develop. Brad has tried on several occasions to exercise and eat right. He is successful until the stress level at work increases. Then the pounds come right back on.

Brad has hired a health coach to help him become healthy again.

What are the key issues Brad is addressing? What requests would you make of him?

- The real issue is not weight. Weight is the presenting issue. I would want to hear more and ask him what the real issue is.
- It is important to notice that what the person wants to be coached in the beginning may not be the real issue.

How would you coach Brad?

- In an attempt to understand the bigger picture and the real issue, I would ask Brad to talk about other issues similar to his weight challenge.
- Most health coaches deal with the whole person. The health coach would see that it is not a matter of health, it is something else. He would ask: what do you want your next 50 years to look like? What do you want to be able to say about yourself in the years to come?

What, if any, tools and resources would you use with him?

- Brad would be a great candidate for the 10 daily habits to help him feel better and reduce stress. This could give him options for not going to the fridge.

Scenario #3: Carol — Senior Manager, Global Organization

Carol is burned out in her current position as senior manager for the global team of organizational development trainers. She has worked in this position for ten years. Because of the global structure, Carol's job requires many extra hours every week outside of normal US business hours to support her team members in other countries. In addition, a peer who used to lead the Curriculum Development Team recently left, and Carol is leading that team in the interim. The result is that she has little time or energy for developing her team or working toward strategic goals of the team, both of which she will be held accountable for in her year-end performance evaluation. In addition, her personal life is virtually non-existent, as she has no time for family and friends. Carol's complaints are that she has lost the passion for her job, she feels overwhelmed and, in general, her life is lacking fun. She is considering leaving the position.

At the same time, Carol is not confident she will be able find another position that allows her as much flexibility, autonomy, and the ability to work from home. She is, in many ways, her own boss.

In spite of being overwhelmed and the lack of passion and fun, Carol is considering pursuing a job opening at another organization. She recognizes she is full of contradictions and seems unable to make any decisions regarding this entire situation. How would you coach Carol?

What is great about Carol? What are her strengths?

- She is really dedicated to what she does and is very respected. She also has strong leadership skills.
- She is respected, responsible, and an outstanding leader.

What questions would you ask Carol?

- What is possible here?
- What is the simplest way to move forward?
- What are the most outrageous next steps she could take?

What are some requests you anticipate that you would make?

- I want her to give herself permission to explore new jobs, as well as to establish stronger boundaries in her current job.

- Since in many ways she is her own boss, she is in charge of how she uses her time and what she focuses on. I would request that she ask the same of herself as she does of others that she supervises.

- I would also request that she have fun—even if she has to schedule it.

Scenario #4: Bob – Vice President of Training and Quality

Bob has been Vice President of Training and Quality for two years at ABC Organization. When Bob first arrived at ABC, he began to implement a new quality approach designed to improve the customer interaction. Bob's approach to developing a strong quality process was to develop service metrics along with training and development for employees in support of those metrics. In addition, he requested that the operations team's supervisors and managers listen to two calls per month for each team member using a standardized call form. He faced a bit of opposition originally, especially from the vice president of operations in the Southeast region. Bob's predecessor had not requested the operations team be a part of the quality process. At this point, the customer quality has not moved up as much as Bob had anticipated and the operations VPs are questioning whether their supervisors have enough time to evaluate two calls per month per team member. The quality team is finding several ways to improve the process and impact the customer positively, and customer satisfaction results are improving drastically. Bob believes it is imperative that the operations team is actively supporting these efforts in order for quality and customer satisfaction to improve.

The last conversation Bob had with the three VPs of operations was difficult. At the conclusion of the meeting, the VP of Operations for the Southeast region indicated he was not participating in the process any longer. Bob feels strongly about his quality process and has the data to back up his argument to keep moving forward with this process for at least another six months to see how the results are over a 12-month cycle. Bob has requested a meeting with the COO and the three VPs of Operations to make a final decision about the quality process.

Bob believes this quality process is the best way to move the needle on customer satisfaction, he has seen it work in another organization where he led the quality efforts and he is seeing incremental success at ABC. He knows the upcoming meeting will be difficult and he needs to maintain the relationship with the VPs of Operations. He wonders if he is really cut out to be a vice president. He wonders if it is time to give up the quality process as a standard approach and just work with the two VPs that are still interested, or should he just let operations lead the efforts as it was done previously.

Bob comes to coaching requesting to gain clarity around his decision and come away with a plan for the meeting.

What more do you want to know from Bob, if anything?

- As a general rule, I like to invite those that I coach to "tell me more." Often, the simple act of "telling more" helps the coachee to gain clarity.

- Another option would be to invite Bob to brainstorm various ways that he can approach this, along with their impact on the outcome. In a way, you would be asking Bob to do a 360-degree view of his current situation.

- It might also be helpful for Bob to let the data drive the next steps, versus having Bob or another VP decide. This removes the individuals from the decision and places it squarely on the data. The hope would be to remove "ego" from the conversation.

- Questions to ask would include:
  - What are the others seeing that you are not seeing?
  - What can you glean from the dissenting VP? What is he seeing from his vantage point?
  - What, if anything, is more important that this issue?

What do you want for Bob?

- I want for Bob to see the whole picture and gather different perspectives.
- Using the Head-Heart-Hunch Coaching Model, I want Bob to increase Head and Heart in this situation. He naturally brings Head, since he works with facts. Bringing a balance of Head-Heart- Hunch would provide Bob with a shift in perspective and possible new awareness.

What, if any, tools would you use?

- A 360-degree Evaluation of Bob. This would provide Bob with a total picture of his leadership and how he is perceived.

- An Emotional Intelligence Assessment. This would help Bob to gain greater clarity about how he relates to others.

- S.W.O.T. Analysis of the current situation. Strengths. Weaknesses. Opportunities. Threats.

Scenario #5: Molly – New Promotion

Molly was recently promoted to Vice President of Operations, following the dismissal of the previous VP who was well received among his team, yet did not get results. The dismissal was unexpected and has caused much unrest within the team, with clients, and among her peers. Molly was transferred from another location with the expectation of stabilizing the team and getting the results needed to keep the site productive.

In your last session with Molly, she indicated she was excited about the new opportunity, yet well aware of the work that lies ahead for her. She is committed to helping this team be successful, but confides in you that, while she believes she can positively impact both the team and the results, she finds herself feeling sad and stressed. Molly finds she has to manage her time differently now that she is a site leader and must juggle client, corporate, and team expectations. She really believes she needs to focus on the site team and processes in order to stabilize the team and get the results everyone wants, yet she finds herself being pulled in many different directions. In addition, Molly believes she needs to manage expectations, especially those of her boss and primary client, but she really doesn't know where to start, and those are key relationships that she must keep intact. She mentions she isn't on track with her monthly financial or metrics goals.

Outline your approach/strategy with Molly.

What do you see the key issues as being and how would you coach Molly?

- One key issue is the stress that she derives from the expectations of people.

- Molly is juggling multiple things at once. I want Molly to stop juggling and do one thing at a time, and focus on what she is good at.

- I want Molly to shift from what others want to what she really, really wants.

What questions would you ask Molly?

- What do you really, really want?
- What is the 40,000-foot view?

- What's the simplest next step?

- What's the real issue?

- Who can help you with this?

- What does success look like ...

  - This week?

  - 30 days from now?

  - 6 months from now?

  - 18 months from now?

Scenario #6: Ethan — Derailing Behavior

Ethan is having difficulty in the area of people development. He does a great job as a leader with his administrative duties and consistently completes tasks and meets client demands, mostly at the expense of his team and his personal time. Ethan has not yet learned how to coach and develop his team, and he often finds difficulty delegating and supporting his team as they lead projects.

In his 360 assessments, he received feedback that he doesn't delegate well, provides little to no direction on projects, and generally doesn't spend time coaching and developing his team. Ethan is devastated; his supervisor has requested he work with one of the organization's internal coaches to determine how to best move forward. Ethan has requested a meeting with you to work on his coaching and development skills.

Outline your approach/strategy with Ethan.

What do you see the key issues as being and how would you coach Ethan?

- Ethan's response to the 360 is interesting. He was "devastated." This seems to be an area of significant development.

- I would also want to know how Ethan processes new information and feedback, such as this. I want to provide him the opportunity to fully process the results of his recent 360.

- Since Ethan didn't decide to work with a coach on his own, I want to know how ready and willing he is to be coached. I would want to hear a readiness on his part to fully participate in the coaching process.

What would be the most challenging part of coaching Ethan?

- Moving him from "enrollment" to "choice" regarding coaching. Unless he is willing to fully engage in the coaching process, the coaching can't move forward. Initially, I think that he is ready to be coached. My concern is further along in the process. I want him to be at a place of choice throughout the coaching process.

What are some requests you anticipate that you would make?

- Stay fully engaged in the coaching process. I'd probably want to have him agree to a minimum number of coaching sessions; i.e., nine months of coaching, twice per month.

- Repeat the 360 Assessment six to nine months into the coaching process.

- Request that Ethan take an Emotional/Social Intelligence Questionnaire. This would add an additional dimension to the coaching conversation for Ethan.

Scenario #7: Julie – Director of a Non-Profit

Julie, a director of a non-profit, relies heavily on her small, salaried staff and several regular committed volunteers. She is forthright in letting all her workers know how much their work is appreciated. One of Julie's joys is developing those around her in addition to the actual work of the non-profit. For Julie, this job is closely aligned with what she believes is her life purpose.

There are several challenges Julie faces. It is hard to maintain enough workers to keep the non-profit open the number of hours the governing body would like. Due to the nature of the non-profit, Julie must carefully screen her workers to be sure they meet the background requirements and are in agreement with the non-profit's purpose. The public relationship of the non-profit is key to its success; support from the community is critical to its survival.

After several years in her position, a new and troubling situation has occurred. Someone in the community reported to the governing body a situation that involved one of the volunteers. The situation is neither illegal nor in direct conflict with the non-profit. The governing body instructed Julie to not allow that volunteer to participate.

Julie says she is devastated at the prospect of "firing" a volunteer. Julie is concerned about the effect this will have on the volunteer and some in the community if it becomes public. She feels either the person who reported the situation or the rejected volunteer could easily blow this out of proportion. This has been keeping Julie awake at night and has her very upset, to the point of thinking about resigning.

Julie says she wants to know what to do.

What questions would you ask Julie?

- What are your options?
- Ten years from now when you look back on this, what do you want to be able to say about how you dealt with this?
- Who can help you with this?
- What's the real issue?
- Instead of viewing this as "firing a volunteer," how else can you view this?
- Tell me more …

What do you hear in Julie's account of this situation?

- I hear worry and concern. For the volunteer, the organization, and the community.
- Julie did not say how she wants to resolve this situation. I want to hear her thoughts. What are her suggestions?
- I heard her passion and energy for this organization and the work that it does. I also heard even greater passion and energy for the staff and volunteers.
- Julie derives much personal value and esteem from her involvement in this organization.

Scenario #8: Steve – Organizational Leader

Steve is a new client who is struggling to meet the commitments he makes in his coaching sessions. He has been working with you for about 90 days. In your last call he committed to several tasks. As you begin the call, he announces he has had a horrible week and he did not stay on top of the agreed upon tasks.

Steve tells you he believes that he will likely end up dropping out of the 12-month accelerated leadership program. His life is too busy with his new promotion, the impending reorganization, and the rollout of a new, key product. He also indicates that he is questioning whether he really wants to stay at this company and he isn't sure he is interested in being on the "accelerated leader" track. (This is very different from your initial conversations with him.)

He then shares he has gotten some feedback from the facilitators in his accelerated leadership program that his collaboration and conflict management skills are opportunities for development. This is the first time he has received feedback of that nature. He really is quite worried about the development required in this program given everything else on his plate at the moment. He also makes a side comment that he doesn't like all the presentations required in this program or his new position – he never really was comfortable speaking in front of others. He ends with a statement about how he really doesn't see the value of the accelerated leadership program; maybe he should drop out and focus on the important, priority items, like running the business and getting results.

What questions do you have of Steve?

- I would like to know what is really going on. What's the real issue?

- What changed?

- I might also ask:

  - Which Steve should I believe? Current Steve – considering dropping out. Or, the Initial Steve – excited and eager to develop as a leader.

- I'd also ask if this is usual for Steve. Hot-cold outlook and behavior.

What does Steve need from his coach?

- Encouragement to stay in the coaching and accelerated leadership process.

- A Mirror. He needs his coach to accurately reflect back to Steve not only the present, but also hopes and dreams. In addition, he needs his coach to hold his feet to the fire so that he remains steadfast.

- To see his recent feedback in a different light. To see feedback as healthy and helpful.

Summary

This section reviewed several coaching scenarios that are common in today's coaching. There are a multitude of other possible scenarios, and it is important to remember these are generalizations. Being curious, exploring strengths, defining vision, exploring options, and aligning with our individual coachees are all important parts to powerful coaching. Each situation is as different as the people that come for coaching. Coaching is not about consulting or prescribing a plan. Coaching is about bringing out the best in our clients and those around them.

Chapter Four

Coaching Intact Teams and Groups

As with individuals, coaching for teams and groups can be a transformational tool for forward progress and performance. Employing coaching skills with groups and teams provides a powerful way for teams to achieve results and capitalize on the collective strengths of the group.

Leaders who use a coach approach generally find their team members are more engaged, solutions are of a higher quality, and there is more buy-in to solutions and the execution of those solutions. Teams using a coach approach generally share leadership, responsibility and accountability in a more productive manner. Coaching is a powerful way to develop the skills of team members and to build up future leaders.

Leaders who use a coach approach with their teams and groups generally find that they lead with questions versus statements or directives, and look for the answers within the group versus providing the answers to the group. Coaching leaders promote action and accountability on an individual and team level, and spend more time listening and less time talking. Coaching leaders view their role as "catalyst" versus "designer."

Understanding the stages of development of a team or group can be useful in coaching teams; the stages of team development can provide clues that explain team behavior. Dr. Bruce Tuckman developed the Five Stages of Team Dynamics. These include:

1. Forming
2. Storming
3. Norming
4. Performing
5. Adjourning (in the 1970s)

Another approach to understanding team development is to view the team from the human development perspective. This approach would include the following stages of development:

- Childhood

- Adolescence

- Young Adulthood

- Middle Adulthood

- Seasoned Adulthood

Forming/Childhood. At this stage the team is relatively new. Individuals are just beginning to get to know each other as they work toward their identity as a group. Generally, the group avoids controversy and decisions as they attempt to develop relationships and identity.

As the coach, your job is to put them at ease and create a safe space. Encourage the team to make decisions and be open to having in-depth discussions and communicating candidly and respectfully. When working with the team, employ your questioning and active listening skills, work with the group to clarify goals, and help the team identify individual roles and responsibilities. Lastly, encourage and support the process of building trust among team members.

Storming/Adolescence. This is the stage of development where team members begin to "jockey" for positions and roles on the team. During this stage, team members can become disillusioned and often "check out" of the group when competition and conflict begin to occur. The group is working on how they will handle conflict and is beginning to understand the personalities and strengths of each team member.

As the coach, one of your roles is to help the team traverse the rocky path of becoming a fully functioning team. Work with the team to resolve conflict effectively and make decisions as a team. In this stage, coaches will continue to help team members establish their role on the team and support others in doing the same. It is not uncommon for team members to challenge each other and the leader. As a coach, help them do this in a manner that is conducive to developing and maintaining working relationships. Use your acknowledging skills and look for the strengths and points of agreement.

Norming/Young Adulthood. During this stage in the process, the team's ability to collaborate effectively increases. Trust begins to fully develop among team members. The team is receptive to new ideas as well as the ideas of others—both inside and outside the team. The team discusses and develops its processes and working style. Agreement and consensus begin to emerge within the team. Roles and responsibilities become clearer and "big" decisions are often made by group collaboration. Smaller decisions may be delegated to individuals or small teams within the group.

As the coach, encourage the team to work together to explore alternatives and work on solutions within established team ground rules. In this stage, coaches may want to take a step back and let the team begin to work more independently. Your role is to partner with the team to help them reach their fullest potential. Keep the team on task and encourage them to engage in fun and social activities.

Performing/Middle Adulthood. In this stage the team has learned how to tap into the strengths of each team member. The team members show loyalty, trust and openness. The team exhibits a high level of creativity and productivity. Differences in opinion are viewed as a springboard for innovation.

The team is strategically focused in its shared vision and is clear about what needs to be accomplished. The team has a high degree of autonomy. Disagreements occur and are now resolved within the team in a positive manner. Team members look after each other and need very little direction from the leader.

As the coach, acknowledge and praise team members on their accomplishments and encourage them to do the same with each other. At this stage your role will evolve into more of an "ad hoc" resource to the team. Take time out to evaluate team effectiveness and encourage team members to do the same individually and within the team. Look for coaching opportunities to support the team in achieving peak performance.

Adjourning/Seasoned Adulthood. This stage usually occurs when a team has a finite life. When this stage occurs, the team recognizes the project is near completion and the team will disband soon. It can be bittersweet for team members.

As the coach, help the team process what they have learned and accomplished. Work with the team to identify and capitalize on what has been achieved, and how they can move forward with their new knowledge. Encourage the team to celebrate, recognizing that some team members may find this transition difficult.

A few years ago, I was working with an intact organizational team to introduce coaching into their organization as a leadership tool. During the coaching workshop, a coaching session occurred with the vice-president (their leader), and a shift began to occur as the leader and the team began to share their perspectives on the team's working relationship. The vice president candidly shared his thoughts, beliefs, feelings and desires on how he views his team and their success, as did the team. The coaching that happened that afternoon has taken the team from storming straight into norming and given them a strong foundation for performing. Not only was awareness created but forward action was discussed, and a new way of interacting and working together began to develop. This is an example of the power of group coaching.

Creating Awareness with Teams

In coaching we know the importance of creating awareness so forward progress and results can occur. One way to create awareness is with distinctions. A distinction is two words or phrases that are similar in meaning, yet convey subtle but powerful differences. Distinctions can help shift our thinking, which produces different behaviors that lead to different (usually better) results. A few key distinctions to be aware of when coaching teams and groups:

- Working hard vs. producing results
- A team of individuals vs. a team that is connected
- Definition by challenge vs. definition by vision
- Efficient vs. effective
- Adversarial thinking vs. strategic thinking

As coaches, when working with teams, we often need to coach the leaders. The following are shifts leaders may want to consider as they lead their teams:

Shift 1: From Diagnosing to Developing

- Learn to help others develop versus diagnosing and solving their problems.
- Coach them to diagnose their problems and then partner with them to develop and support their progress forward.

Shift 2: From Doing to Empowering

- Leaders must stop doing so others can start doing.
- Empower and develop others to "do."

Shift 3: From Telling to Exploring

- Move from "telling" to "asking."
- Explore possibilities and support them in moving forward on their own.

Shift 4: From Mindlessness to Mindfulness

- Transactional interactions to transformational interactions.
- Being aware and intentional with those you lead.

Shift 5: From Excellence to Effectiveness

- Ready, FIRE, aim to ready, AIM, fire
- Doing something well versus making a difference

Shift 6: From Professional to Entrepreneur

- Status quo to change catalyst
- Risk adverse to embracing risk
- Taking it forward

In coaching it is imperative that we understand the WHO of a group before we move to the WHAT and HOW. As you listen for the WHO of the group, notice the values and beliefs held by the group. Listen for the group's story (without getting hooked into their story or letting it stray too far from the goal). Avoid the tendency to coach the individual team members; stay focused on the team as a whole. Ask:

- What are 10 things I absolutely need to know about this team in order to coach you?
- What do you want to be able to say about yourself as a team?
- What stage of development is this group? (See above information on the stages of team development.)
- What should I never, ever ask or request of this group?
- If this group suddenly disbanded, who would notice? What wouldn't get done?

The following are two resources you can use to successfully coach teams and groups.

Work the Gap

Here and Now vs. Then and There

- Request that the group or team develop a current and realistic picture.
- Request that the group also create a future, ideal picture.
- Ask the group to identify the gap that exists between the current and future picture.

- Begin developing a plan of action to bridge the gap.

- Identify sabotage—when, where and how does sabotage usually show up.

- Create a system of accountability and follow-up to ensure a plan of action is implemented.

Three Questions Model

- What's happening in this group? (Current reality picture.)

- What's possible in this group? (Put on your rose colored glasses.)

- What steps can we take to move forward as a group? (Today. Right now.)

Coaching teams is much like a juggling act—several balls in the air at once. The goal is to keep all the balls moving so the art of juggling can be accomplished. Similarly in teams, the coach keeps everyone moving forward so the team can perform at peak performance.

Chapter Five

Creating New Awareness

Beliefs and assumptions are not necessarily good or bad. Everyone has beliefs and assumptions that are 100% true for those who believe them. There are usually stories, history and/or background that support the beliefs and assumptions individuals have about themselves, others and/or situations. These beliefs and assumptions show up in coaching all the time. Our job as a coach is to bring them to the surface so they can be explored, understood, put into perspective, and/or put to rest. Beliefs and assumptions can:

- Propel us forward OR paralyze us.

- Expand our options OR limit our choices.

- Rally one to take initiative OR cause one to throw in the towel.

Belief—A certainty or truth accepted by an individual or a group.

Assumption—Believed to be true without proof, or the proof is situational or circumstantial.

Many times our limiting beliefs and false assumptions are nothing more than F.E.A.R.— "False Emotions Appearing Real." As a coach, listen for limiting beliefs and false assumptions; this is a way to help those you coach determine the underlying, important issue. You will find limiting beliefs and false assumptions show up in a diverse manner. As coaches we need to be on the lookout so we can surface these beliefs and assumptions and work with the coaches to create awareness.

We all have limiting beliefs and false assumptions; some are known to us while others lie just below the surface, waiting to be known. When we scratch below the surface of what the person is saying, we often uncover and bring to the surface limiting beliefs and false assumptions. Limiting beliefs and false assumptions are the core of the inner recording that has been created in our minds.

A few examples of beliefs and assumptions:

- The world is flat!

- Nothing ever really changes.

- They will think that I'm stupid.

- I don't know as much as they do.

- I can't do that job.

- We really don't have a choice.

- Change is always difficult.

- Change takes time.

- I cannot lead.

- We're not as big as the XYZ organization.

Techniques to Uncover Limiting Beliefs and False Assumptions

- **Be Curious and Inquisitive.** Limiting beliefs and false assumptions have gained power because they have gone unquestioned.

- **Ask Open-Ended, Powerful Questions** that go below the surface to the limiting beliefs and false assumptions.

- **Express Appreciation.** A 5 to 1 ratio of appreciation to criticism helps people think creatively (*Time to Think*, by Nancy Kline). Change takes place best in a context of genuine praise. Look for the greatness in individuals rather than trying to fix everyone.

- **Invite Others to Engage Their Mind.** Request that they play and have fun. Play engages curiosity. A person who is having fun is more likely to experiment. As we age, curiosity tends to decrease. In a recent study, 870 children were tracked regarding curiosity at age 6 and then again at age 16. At 8 years of age, 84% of the children were in curiosity mode; at 16 years of age, 7% of the children were in curiosity mode. Over a span of 8 years most children stop being curious.

As a coach, our job is to find the best way to surface limiting beliefs and false assumptions and encourage curiosity as a way to work though the process of eliminating our limiting beliefs and false assumptions.

How Beliefs and Assumptions are Formed

- **Early Childhood Experiences.** Experiences in the first seven years of life can have a large affect on the view of an individual's world.

- **Family Environment.** Parents, school and the community an individual is exposed to play a part in shaping their belief system. How an individual encounters difficulties is largely determined by the experience they have encountered as a child.

- **Modeling.** This refers to unconsciously taking on the beliefs, opinions, and perspectives of someone deeply admired. The viewpoint of their model is often taken on as their own viewpoint, with very little questioning.

- **Significant Experiences.** Life-altering experiences shape an individual's beliefs. If the experiences turn out to be successful, the individual is likely to believe anything is possible. If the experiences are unsuccessful and the attitude is negative, the individual is likely to adopt thoughts and fears, which impede empowerment and belief in self.

As a coach, don't be afraid to use your powerful questioning techniques as a means to challenge those you coach when you find a limiting belief and/or false assumption. At times it may be appropriate to ask for permission to "go down a certain path" with a line of questions. It will be important for you to determine how you need to proceed as you uncover and seek to create awareness with those you coach. Your coaching relationship, as well as your personal style, will play a large part in determining how you challenge those you coach.

Beliefs and Assumptions Shape Our Worldview

Beliefs and assumptions determine how individuals view their world and act as a confirmation of reality. In essence, they play a part in shaping worldview. Problems occur when beliefs and assumptions are flawed, distorted or steeped in unhelpful ways. Only when an individual becomes consciously aware of their limiting beliefs and false assumptions, can there be the possibility of change occurring.

The human mind is powerful, and in many cases our thinking becomes our reality. Positive beliefs and assumptions usually lead to positive outcomes, while limiting beliefs and false assumptions tend to produce negative outcomes and/or get in the way of positive forward movement. When individuals are attached to their limiting beliefs and/or false assumptions that they cannot do something, they operate from that perspective, thereby sabotaging their efforts for success. In addition, they prevent themselves from finding evidence to disprove those limiting beliefs and/or false assumptions.

When thoughts impede empowerment, individuals get worn down and find themselves in a constant struggle. Instead of a smooth, easy path, these individuals find themselves facing many difficulties. Limiting beliefs and false assumptions thwart the process of personal growth. To dispel limiting beliefs and false assumptions, it is crucial to deal with self-sabotaging thoughts and determine their origin. Next, we must understand their impact on forward progress and determine how to reframe and move forward differently. The life we live is largely determined by our beliefs and assumptions.

Generally speaking, when limiting beliefs and false assumptions are deeply rooted, they usually show up in the form of black or white thinking. This simply means there is a tendency to think in "either/or" and/or extreme terms, such as "should" and "should never," "can" and "cannot," "possible" and "impossible," and "never" and "always." Individuals become victims in life when they refuse to let go of their negative thoughts.

- In the face of a financial disaster, an individual believes they are not worthy of having money.

- When someone finds himself or herself having difficulty finding friends, their perception becomes "no one loves me" or "it is hard to make friends."

- When an individual encounters problems at work, they say "I am not good enough."

These are all examples of how limiting beliefs and false assumptions occur.

Incisive Questioning

As coaches, our goal is to help those we coach see themselves differently and, then, behave according to that new perspective. In her book *Time to Think*, Nancy Kline offers a simple yet profound method for dealing with limiting beliefs and false assumptions. Her method involves asking the incisive questions as you attempt to open up, surface and address limiting beliefs and false assumptions. As coaches, consider the following process to address limiting beliefs and false assumptions:

STEP 1—Ask the coachee to articulate the goal, dream and desired outcome.

- For themselves and, if applicable, for others and the situation.
- Help them get clarity about what they really, REALLY want to accomplish.
- Get them to define what they want—create a vision.
- What do they want to be able to say 3, 6, 9, or 12 months from now?
- As Covey says, "Begin with the end in mind." (Covey 1999, 237)

STEP 2—What beliefs and/or assumptions are barriers to the goal, dream and desired outcome?

- Get to the core issue regarding beliefs and/or assumptions about this goal.
- Ask about the reasons the individual or group hasn't achieved their goal(s).

- Identify obstacles, especially beliefs and assumptions that have kept them from moving forward.

- Look for patterns/trends that might be supporting limiting beliefs and false assumptions.

STEP 3—Articulate the POSITIVE OPPOSITE of the current situation.

- This is often a difficult task for an individual or team to do, but press them to articulate the positive opposite.

- Once articulated, ask them to write it down and get them to talk about it—what it would look like, feel like, be like, etc.

- Ask "If you knew <insert the Positive Opposite>, what action would you take? What would be different?"

STEP 4—Write down the action you will take.

- Ask the coachee to design actions to achieve the positive opposite.

- Discuss obstacles and challenges.

- Capitalize on the momentum of the conversation.

- Find out what support they need to make the change.

As you consider beliefs and assumptions, challenge your coachee to view them differently and/or think about them from the other viewpoint. Ask them to consider the following. What if:

- You no longer held these beliefs/assumptions?

- These beliefs/assumptions were no longer true?

- You decided to consider other options/beliefs/viewpoints?

- For today, you let go of "X" (limiting belief/false assumption) and believed "Y" (positive opposite)?

- Going forward you acted/behaved/believed in a manner that supported the positive opposite of your limiting belief/false assumption. How would you show up? What might occur?

And sometimes you just have to keep trying, according to an often shared story about Abraham Maslow regarding the power of beliefs. One of his patients refused to eat because he believed he was a corpse. In exasperation, the psychiatrist finally asked him if corpses bled. The patient said he did not believe so. Maslow then proceeded to prick him with a pin (after asking permission). At which point, the patient started to bleed. In amazement, the patient declared, "Wow…corpses do bleed after all."

Challenging Limiting Beliefs and False Assumptions

Once you have uncovered limiting beliefs and false assumptions, the next step is to go about challenging and changing those beliefs to incorporate a new approach to the situation. Change is always difficult—even when it is positive. Change requires individuals to prepare, think and act differently, which not only has a personal impact but also an impact on relationships. Change produces a chain reaction in our lives.

In coaching, creating awareness is only half the equation; taking action and accountability is the other half. Similarly, with limiting beliefs and false assumptions, it is not enough to surface and understand them, the coachee must move forward differently in order to achieve a sustainable, positive outcome.

> AWARENESS + ACTION + ACCOUNTABILITY = SUSTAINABLE CHANGE

As a coach, one of our roles is to affect change by asking our coachees to step out of their comfort zones and support them in making room for their new perspective.

When someone challenges an individual's limiting beliefs and/or false assumptions, or an individual is given opposing feedback, help them consider how they receive the information. Help those you coach be open to seeing things differently and/or exploring how they might see things from a different perspective. Challenge them to put themselves in the other person's shoes and take a look from that perspective. Ask them to reframe their thinking and identify the silver lining in the situation. Help them articulate and identify their learning opportunities and determine what is true and what is false.

Many beliefs and assumptions have served individuals well in the past, kept them successful and/or contributed to a healthy and productive lifestyle. When working in this capacity as a coach, ask them to reconsider those beliefs and assumptions in light of the current situation. The question becomes "Is this belief or assumption still useful for you?" If you can create thoughts, you can definitely change them.

I often coach individuals in organizations who are deemed "high potential." My work with this group usually involves some activities around creating awareness. In most instances, the goal is to unlock potential and accelerate performance, which oftentimes is about creating awareness of gifts and/or limiting beliefs. In some instances, high potential individuals find themselves exhibiting "derailing behavior" as they transition to the next level and/or a new position. Derailing behavior might show up in the form of a skill that served them well at one level but now is less important at their new level. When this occurs, creating new awareness is key to helping the individual move forward successfully.

Here is another example. In Sarah's younger days, her family taught her to "pinch your pennies" because there was never enough money to feed the family. Into adulthood, she continues to hold on to the belief that resources are scarce, even though it is not truly the case in her present situation. She becomes selfish and miserly, always counting the pennies. This feeling of scarcity also affects her ability to give love, friendship and support, because she suffers from a sense of "lacking" in her life.

As you work with those you coach, when you find a tendency for someone to hold on to a limiting belief and/or false assumption, it could signify something they perceive of value is making it difficult for them to release the limiting belief and/or false assumption. Dig deeper until you find the cause!

One of my favorite quotes is from the Eagles' song "Already Gone." As a coach it is our job to help our clients find their "key."

> "So oftentimes it happens, that we live our life in chains. And we never even know we have the key."
> — The Eagles, *Already Gone*

Chapter Six

Establishing Yourself as a Coach

If you have gotten this far in your journey, you have experienced the power of coaching both in your own life and as you have sought to coach others. Now you are standing on the edge asking "What's next?"

Next, for many, will be incorporating coaching into your current professional scenarios, or creating a coaching culture within your organization. For others, next is transitioning to a full-time coach. Many of those I have coached have viewed this next step as next to impossible—almost like a Grand Canyon-size gap between where they are and where they want to be.

This section has been created to help you traverse the Grand Canyon. The information contained in this chapter is a compilation of years of coaching, mentor-coaching and coach-training. While it is not an exhaustive resource, it is a collection of best practices, strategies and shifts to help you successfully establish yourself as a coach.

Let's begin with a checklist. The following checklist is designed to give you a quick snapshot of how you are doing, as well as to identify what is needed. The checklist below will help you gain an accurate picture of your current reality.

ITEM	YES	NO
I am able to say "I am a coach!" with a straight face.		
I have identified 4 to 7 connectors (i.e., people that know how to make things happen), who have agreed to help me build my coaching business.		
I am working with a mentor-coach who has their own successful, sustainable, coaching business.		
I am comfortable talking to others about money.		
I have a financial reserve and a financial plan.		
I know coaching is legitimate, even if people don't get it.		
I have set up a coaching environment so I am fully present with those I coach.		
I have a good headset, computer and internet service.		

ITEM	YES	NO
I have a back-up telephone or mobile phone.		
I am ready to coach (i.e., I have a professional looking welcome letter, website, business cards, coaching agreement and payment process) and I have automated this as much as possible.		
I regularly follow up with prospective and previous coachees.		
BONUS—I regularly celebrate my successes, no matter how small or large.		

Based on your answers above consider the following:

- How well positioned are you to start coaching?

- What are you doing well?

- Where do you need to focus more time and effort?

- In 12 months, what do you want to be able to say that you cannot say now?

Typical Transition Strategies

As you think about starting a coaching business, consider the different ways that people enter a swimming pool. Some people jump right in, while others ease their way into the water. Still others never leave the kiddie pool. How do you enter a swimming pool?

Just as there are different ways to enter a pool, there are different ways to transition into coaching. Consider the following approaches. Ask yourself which one is best for you. What are the implications of your approach? What are the benefits of each approach?

Jump into the Deep End of the Pool. Jump right in!

- Quit your job and start a coaching practice, or

- Get a no brainer job so you can focus on coaching.

Slide into the Pool. First your big toe, then slowly enter the pool.

- Work full-time and coach part-time.

- Eventually work part-time and coach part-time.

- Gradually add more and more clients.

Bring the Pool to You. Incorporate coaching into your current position.

- Talk to your employer, supervisor or board about incorporating coaching into what you already do.

- Develop an internal coaching position.

- Bloom right where you are planted.

Swim in Someone Else's Pool. Partner, collaborate or join another coach's team.

- Work for another coach.

- Pool your resources with other coaches.

When I considered starting my own coaching business, I employed a few of the strategies simultaneously. I begin my coach training in the corporate environment and "brought the pool to me," as I incorporated coaching into my current position. My current corporate position eventually led to leading the internal coaching team. Simultaneous to my work in the corporate environment, I used the "swim in someone else's pool" and the "slide into the pool" approach, as I developed my own business on the side and partnered with other seasoned coaches. When the time was right I was positioned well to transition to full-time coaching. The combination of these approaches allowed me to gain experiences, expertise and partnerships, which provided a foundation that supported the end goal of owning my own coaching practice.

Begin at the End

Begin with the end in mind. It's not uncommon for a new coach to forget about developing a complete vision of their coaching business. We coach others to begin with a clear picture of the end. Without a bull's-eye on the target, how will you know if you have been successful?

Consider the following series of questions as one way of gaining greater clarity as to the purpose of your coaching business, as well as painting the picture and defining what your business looks like.

- How do you define full-time coaching?

- What would an ideal week (or month) look like for you as a full-time coach?

- Describe the ideal individual or team that you are coaching.

- What are your beliefs and assumptions about full-time coaching?

- Of the beliefs you have identified, which are limiting you? Which are serving you well? What new beliefs do you want to add?

• Where are you in the process of transitioning to full-time coaching? What are the next two or three key steps?

The Upside-Down Funnel Approach

Most people, when launching a business, adopt the "Funnel Approach." This approach, like a funnel, is wide at the top and narrow at the bottom. Using this approach, an individual attempts to contact, connect, network and market to as many people and organizations as possible. This approach attempts to touch a large number of people (wide end of the funnel) and usually yields a few people (narrow end of the funnel).

The "Upside-Down Funnel Approach" literally inverts the traditional approach. Instead of a mass approach, which is very impersonal, this approach advocates connecting with a much smaller group and investing in them. All that is needed in this approach are four to seven really good "connectors." Investing heavily in a few people (narrow end of the funnel) yields much (wide end of the funnel).

Who are connectors and where do you find them? Connectors are individuals who know how to make things happen. Every organization has them. These are the Paul Reveres versus the William Dawes from our history books. Both of these individuals were asked to spread the word about impending danger. People listened to Paul and paid little attention to William.

One of my original connectors brought me 34 coachees all at once. While subsequent connectors haven't delivered this high number at once, they regularly help me secure larger contracts and introduce me to other connectors.

Consider the following strategies:

• **Identify Your Connectors.** Sit down and begin listing names. They are there. Comb through your address book and contact list.

• **Invest in Your Connectors.** Connect with your connectors and develop the relationship further. Add value to their world—value is the currency of their world. I've coached many connectors, done favors for them and worked to help develop them personally and professionally.

• **Be on the Lookout for New Connectors.** Always look for your next connector. Early on I thought connectors had to be people I knew well. That's a myth. Connectors, by their very nature, like expanding their connections. It's what makes them so effective. I have several connectors I have never met in person, who don't really know me, but know another connector who recommended me.

Key Shifts

As a coach, I know about shifts. I coach individuals and teams on key shifts all the time. Shifts are internal (or below the surface) changes and re-orientations that dramatically alter one's approach or perspective, resulting in a significantly different outcome. As a coach, I also have shifts. Consider the following key shifts as you develop your coaching business.

Shift: Hobby vs. Business

Coaching as a hobby is fun, intriguing and interesting. As a hobby, you immerse yourself in coaching when you want to. Making money is optional; in fact, the investment in most hobbies is far greater than the return. And that's okay. It's a hobby.

Coaching as a business is also fun, intriguing and interesting…and more. As a business owner, you are monitoring investment and return. Making money is NOT optional. There are intentional processes and approaches in place to further develop and sustain the business for the benefit of the coach and coachee.

This shift impacts your decision-making process. Decisions now include not only ROI (return on investment) but also your vision from both a personal and business viewpoint. In addition, you will need to consider financial obligations and responsibilities, as well as key partnerships. Lastly, you will need to look at how you make course corrections and process improvements to increase efficiency and remain relevant.

How would you rate yourself regarding this shift?

Hobby <————————————————————————————> Business

Shift: Free-Based Coaching versus Fee-Based Coaching

One of the places many newer coaches have difficulty is charging a fee. For many this is a difficult shift. New coaches want to know the secret of charging a fee, especially when they hear the fee structures of seasoned coaches. Questions abound:

- What's a good coaching fee for a newer coach?
- How do you ask for a fee?
- How do you explain what coaching is?

- And, what about the rejection—how do you handle the dreaded "No"?

Consider the following comments regarding this shift:

- As coaching confidence and competency increases, generally speaking, fees increase.

- Charging a fee for coaching is as much a benefit to the coachee as it is to the coach. Coachees who are financially invested in coaching tend to approach the coaching process very differently than pro-bono coachees. Those who pay for coaching show up prepared and ready to fully engage in the coaching process. They are also much more likely to have taken the agreed upon action steps. Paying coachees are willing to go deeper in the coaching conversation and tend to place a higher value on the coaching process and their coach.

- There are really only four reasons people say NO:
  - NO Need
  - NO Money
  - NO Hurry
  - NO Credibility

    By Ken Abrams (www.kenabrams.com)

- **BONUS: The fifth reason people say NO.** Sometimes when a person says NO, what they are really saying is NOT YET. When we hear them say NO, we stop all contact and follow through. We draw a line through their name and move on to the next person. And that's where it ends. Yet, what is really needed by the prospective coachee is time and space to think and prepare before they are ready to begin the coaching process. They are looking for periodic follow through, additional value and connection.

Skillful listening enables the coach to hear the distinction between NO versus NOT YET. Identifying the value-to-add is part of this process. Discerning the frequency and type of follow-up are critical, as well as listening past the NO. **Follow-through matters.**

Shift: Selling versus Adding Value

A common myth among many newer coaches is that you have to be able to sell in order to have a full-time coaching business. Or, that you have to be an expert at marketing. Nothing could be further from the truth. In fact, my experience has been that traditional sales and marketing approaches do not work and frequently distract newer coaches from investing in steps that will further develop their coaching business.

Rather than selling, this shift is about identifying what's really needed. This shift is about eliminating questions like:

- How do I convince people to purchase what I'm selling?
- How do I get them to want what I'm offering?

Tuned In authors Craig Stull, Phil Myers and David Meerman Scott refer to this as understanding the "Buyer Personas"; in other words, truly understanding who will buy and invest in what you are offering.

> "By truly understanding the market problems your products and services solve for your buyer personas, you transform your marketing from mere product-specific, egocentric gobbledygook that only you understand and care about into valuable information people are eager to consume and that they use to make the choice to do business with your organization." —David Meerman Scott

The "Tuned in Process" is simple to learn and provides a model marketing strategy. (Craig Stull, Phil Myers and David Meerman Scott)

Step 1: Find Unresolved Problems (to know what market and which product or service to focus on).

Step 2: Understand Buyer Personas (to understand who will buy what you are offering).

Step 3: Quantify the Impact (to know if you have a potential winner).

Step 4: Create Breakthrough Experiences (to build a competitive advantage).

Step 5: Articulate Powerful Ideas (to establish the memorable concepts that match up with the problems people have).

Step 6: Establish Authentic Connections (to tell your buyers that you've solved their problems so they buy from you).

Shift: I Am Almost a Coach vs. I Am a Coach

Someone I recently mentor-coached offered the following statement about my success: "The reason you are successful as a coach is because you are sold on the value of your coaching."

See yourself as a coach! The ability to say and believe you are a coach is more important than you think. This is one of those times when a little overconfidence can actually help.

Your Relationship with Money

Strange as it may seem, your relationship with money will impact the success and sustainability of your coaching business. In mentor-coaching, it is common for newer coaches to totally gloss over their current and future financial picture. Another common scenario among newer coaches is to be completely overwhelmed or intimidated by the financial components of a full-time coaching business.

We encourage newer coaches to explore their relationship with money. In many cases newer coaches end up involved in a money makeover regarding their relationship with money. Here are a couple of ways to initiate a money makeover.

- What were your family of origin's beliefs and practices regarding money? How well are these currently serving you?

- What is your current belief about money?

- How well will your current belief about money serve you as you develop a full-time coaching business?

- What new beliefs and practices regarding money do you need to develop?

- How would you define a healthy relationship with money?

- Who do you know who has a healthy relationship with money?

- Take stock of your current financial picture (an honest snapshot):

    - What are your current expenses and income?

    - What are your anticipated expenses? (Remember to include: taxes, health insurance, liability insurance, disability insurance, memberships, etc. Don't forget LLC, incorporation or non-profit status.)

    - How many clients do you need to coach to meet and exceed your expenses?

    - When will your clients pay you? How will they pay you? How much of this can you automate?

- How much financial reserve do you currently have? How much is needed?

- Develop a financial budget and plan. Stick to it. Regularly review it.

How to Speed Things Up

Below is a list of proven best practices for accelerating your transition to full-time coaching:

- Coach, Coach and COACH.

- Connect, Connect and CONNECT.

- Identify your buyer persona (understand who will buy what you are offering).

- Develop a strong personal foundation.

- Rub shoulders with other new coaches who are doing the same thing.

- Identify administrative supports and structures. Remember, you don't have to do it all.

- Decide how and when your coachees will pay for your services.

- Automate as much as possible.

- Before anyone hires you as their coach, create your welcome kit, coaching agreement and prospect letter.

- Have a website and business card in place.

- Will you be creating a newsletter? Hard-copy or email newsletter? Frequency of distribution?

- Hire a mentor-coach.

- Develop relationships with seasoned, successful coaches for mutual support.

- Ahead of time, develop your elevator speech—"I help people get the results they want. I am a coach."

Myths and Mistakes

When developing a full-time coaching business, support is a key ingredient to being successful. Consider the following:

- Family and friends may not regard coaching as a viable business. This can easily discourage a new coach. **Ask for the support and encouragement of your family and friends.**

- At times you will feel overwhelmed, discouraged and stressed by how much you don't know or because the transition is moving along slower than you anticipated. **Work with a mentor-coach! Rub shoulders with other coaches.**

- Stressing yourself financially is a major de-motivator. Even though you may not want to entertain the idea of **keeping your day job**—just do it until you are ready to go solo.

- Identify the people and organizations that you really, REALLY want to coach. Seek them out. **Be selective in who you coach.** Remember, it takes more time to build a practice than you think it should. **Be patient and give yourself time.**

- Realize you're starting a new business, not just getting a new job, starting a hobby or improving yourself. **You are an entrepreneur!** Actually, a "solopreneur."

- You may think that those who know you best will be more likely to hire you or promote your business. Actually, most of our experience has been the exact opposite. **Over 95% of those we coach we have never met before or had a face-to-face meeting.** Plus, those who have been most helpful in building our coaching business have been new connectors whom we have not met in person.

- Identify and address your limiting beliefs and false assumptions about developing a full-time coaching business. Common limiting beliefs include:

  - No one will hire me because…

  - People won't really pay for coaching…

  - I can't…

  - I'm just a…

Chapter Seven

Developing a Solid Personal and Professional Foundation

A strong personal and professional foundation is an intentional decision to live your life in a way that will support you to be your very best (i.e., be at the top of your game). A solid personal and professional foundation is a key ingredient to being your best professionally (i.e., reaching goals, peak performance, as well as valuable contribution to the team, etc).

Using the analogy of a house, your personal and professional foundation is the actual foundation upon which your "house" is built. The foundation is comprised of three main components:

- Your intrapersonal relationship—relationship with yourself.

- Your interpersonal relationship—relationship with others (especially family and friends).

- Your life purpose perspective—your contribution and legacy.

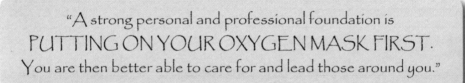

"A strong personal and professional foundation is
PUTTING ON YOUR OXYGEN MASK FIRST.
You are then better able to care for and lead those around you."

GETTING STARTED

As you begin, consider your responses to the following questions:

1. What do you want to be able to say about your personal and professional foundation by the end of this course?

2. Why would this be important to the clients you serve?

3. How do you see this working with the clients you serve?

WHAT'S THE VISION EXERCISE

A strong sense of vision and purpose is what moves us forward in our life. To move forward effectively and with energy, we need to know what we want and have a clear vision on how to get that vision/purpose. Too often, we move through life letting others choose our vision/ purpose or not clearly articulating our personal vision/purpose. This path often robs us of our energy, passion and performance. When working with coachees in developing their vision, purpose, etc., consider the following questions:

- What are your past accomplishments from the last 12 months?

- What are your strengths?

- What is your passion?

- What do you want to say about your future in five years?

- When you think about "who" you are and what you want out of life, what comes to mind?

> A skyscraper doesn't start at street level. In fact, the taller the building, the deeper the foundation.
> This holds true for people too.

- Given the previous question, where are your gaps?

  - What must you address in the next 30 days, the next six months?

  - What are two things you can do immediately to move forward?

- What story do you want to tell?

- Write your personal vision/purpose statement.

> People work ...
> Hard for a paycheck.
> Harder for a person.
> Hardest for a purpose.

Often we are not successful in moving forward because we have competing priorities or are focusing on the "urgent" instead of the "important." It is imperative to have clearly defined goals in order to set up priorities accurately.

The following exercise works well for coachees as they consider their priorities.

PRIORITIES GRID EXERCISE

Consider the tasks, requests, "to dos," etc., in your life and place them in the following grid. Next, evaluate the results of your completed grid and determine your most powerful next steps.

MOST URGENT (Needs immediate attention)	IMPORTANT (A priority)
1. 2. 3.	1. 2. 3.
URGENT AND IMPORTANT (Needs attention and is a priority)	NOT URGENT and NOT IMPORTANT (Does not need immediate attention and is not a priority)
1. 2. 3.	1. 2. 3.

What are your powerful next steps?

THE WHEEL OF LIFE EXERCISE

The Wheel of Life exercise provides a visual representation of how and where you are spending your time. As you build your own wheel of life consider what is important to you - for instance, family, friends, significant other, money, health, career, physical environment, spirituality, fun/recreation, personal growth, education, etc. Then section out your circle and add your own personal life areas. See the sample wheel below.

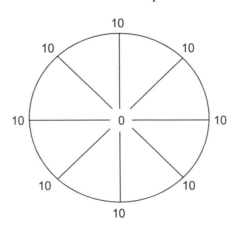

Once you have listed your life areas, the next step is to rate yourself in each of your life areas on a scale of 1 to 10 (1 being the lowest and 10 being the highest). The center of the wheel represents 0 while the outer edge represents 10. Rank your level of satisfaction with each life area by drawing a new "outer edge." The new perimeter of the circle represents your Wheel of Life.

Consider these questions:

- Would the ride be bumpy or smooth if this were a real wheel?

- What two life areas do you want to focus on first?

- Of those two life areas, what are three or four things you can do immediately (in the next 30 days) to increase the satisfaction levels in those areas?

- How will you ensure accountability for the actions you want to take?

TWELVE MONTHS FROM NOW EXERCISE

> What could be worse than being born without sight?
> Being born with sight and no vision.
> ~Helen Keller

Another exercise designed to get your coachee to consider what they want to accomplish over the next 12 months is the "12 Months from Now" exercise. In part one, ask them to write down what they want to say about the past year from the perspective of "looking back" over the last 12 months. Essentially, you are engaging them in future thinking and getting them to define their goals through what they want to say about the past year.

Questions you could ask to generate this type of thinking:

- In part one, write down what you hope to have accomplished over the last 12 months as if you were documenting your accomplishments.

- If you could achieve your goals over the next 12 months, what would that look like?

- What do you want to say about your accomplishments in 12 months?

Once you get your accomplishments documented, then work "backward" to set goals for the next 30 and 60 days in order to achieve those accomplishments. Remember this is a living document and should be updated as goals are achieved and/or as things change.

PART 1: I would like to say the following about the past year...

1. _____

2. _____

3. _____

4. _____

5. _____

PART 2: 30-Day Actions

	Action	Completion Date
1.		
2.		
3.		
4.		
5.		

PART 3: 60-Day Actions

	Action	Completion Date
1.		
2.		
3.		
4.		
5.		

NO MORE TOLERATIONS EXERCISE

If you're only doing it because you feel like you should, then stop SHOULDING on yourself!

Another way to help coachees move forward is to consider what activities are energizing (nurture you, fuel your passion, etc.) and what activities are draining (create physical and emotional stress, pain, tightness, etc.). It is important to consider what you are tolerating that must be handled (i.e., a financial or work-related issue, a stressful relationship, a project that has been on the back burner for too long, etc.).

One way to move forward is to release current habits, tolerations and patterns, which are not focused on fueling passions or moving toward goals. I love to do spring cleaning as it helps eliminate clutter and unnecessary items and opens up space. Similarly, when we release tolerations, we make room for other possibilities and space to just "be." This is often where creativity, shifts and breakthroughs occur.

Take the "clothes closet" theory. To make room for the new, fun clothes, we must rid ourselves of the old, tired clothes! Similarly, to move ourselves forward we must be aggressive in cleaning/clearing our mental house of our drains, tolerations and habits that inhibit us in moving forward positively!

Addressing Tolerations

Consider the following questions to get the conversation started.

- What (or who) are you tolerating right now that is interfering with your personal/professional growth and care?

- What current habits or daily routines are NOT enriching your life?

- How are your boundaries currently working for you?

- Where are your boundaries weak?

- What are ways to dramatically extend your weakest boundaries?

- What needs immediate attention?

- What are you passionate about achieving in the next 90 days?

- What habits/thought processes, etc., must you eliminate to move forward successfully?

- Whose life are you living?

THE C.O.R.E. APPROACH EXERCISE

Another approach to use is the C.O.R.E. Approach—Complete, Outsource, Release, Explore. The C.O.R.E. Approach helps to strengthen position and consider what is not being done.

1. What can I **COMPLETE**? Set deadlines and complete.

Task	Deadline

2. What can I **OUTSOURCE**? Ask for help and/or delegate.

Task	To Whom	By When

3. What can I **RELEASE**? Make a decision to walk away and release (for X amount of weeks/months).

Task	By When

4. What can I **EXPLORE**? What energizes me and will add value to my life?

Idea	By When

FOCUS/REFOCUS EXERCISE

The ability to respond to the challenges of your personal and professional life is no accident. It often includes a realistic understanding of what is actually occurring in the totality of our life. One exercise we find valuable is the Focus/Refocus exercise.

The Focus/Refocus exercise involves taking at look at the following areas and considering how you are performing in your life.

- **Rest Time.** Take care of your physical body. Rest and relaxation.
- **Results Time.** Keep the main things the main things.
- **Response Time.** Ensure adequate time for follow-up and follow-through.
- **Refocus Time.** Schedule time for course corrections and fine-tuning.

The final "R" is the most overlooked. Refocus time is an opportunity to bring things back into balance and to gain a refresh perspective. Refocus time is essential when implementing a new vision or living into your hopes and dreams.

To support coachees in gaining clarity, ask them to respond to each question below. Write down your responses. Consider the following:

- Which category gets the most time?

- Which category gets the least time?

- What is the impact of the answers you gave in questions 1 and 2?

- What does your perfect state look like?

Next consider these questions:

- Who do you need to be in order to make this a reality? (Your perfect state.)

- Identify the specific changes and adjustments necessary.

- What action will you take in the next week? 30 days?

SAYING YES AND NO EXERCISE

When working with coachees on their preferred future it is important to help them understand the when, how and why of saying "yes" and "no" to requests in their life. Consider the Saying Yes and No exercise and help your coachees determine how to move forward according to their stated preferred future. The goal is for the coachee to take a deep dive into their current state, consider what needs to occur, then set action to make that change a reality.

Define the Preferred Future (Goal, Dream, etc):

Based on the preferred future, fill out the following:

I will say YES to the following:

Which means I will say NO to the following:

I will say NO to the following:

So I can say YES to the following:

What are the three most powerful next steps you can take toward your preferred future?

EFFECTIVE HABITS EXERCISE

As we help coachees define vision and purpose, eliminate tolerations, break habits and learn when to say "yes" and "no," we must also address new habits they need to embrace. The Effective Habits exercise will help coachees identify the new habits for success.

> Good habits, once established are just as hard to break as are bad habits. ~Robert Puller

Consider daily and weekly habits in support of your stated goals/choice/vision.

Habit	Daily	Weekly

RED LIGHT/GREEN LIGHT EXERCISE

When moving forward seems daunting, a good activity is the Red Light/Green Light activity. This is designed to provide clarity around the "pros" and "cons" of implementation.

> Nobody ever did, or ever will, escape the consequences of his choices.
> ~Alfred A. Montapert

In this exercise, please consider the pros and cons of implementing and not implementing a particular goal and/or choice. Consider your goal and/or choice from the following four different perspectives.

Please state your goals/choices:

PROS of implementing goals/choices:

CONS of implementing goals/choices:

PROS of **NOT** implementing goals/choices:

CONS of **NOT** implementing goals/choices:

Once complete, discuss with the coachee their answers, their options, and associated consequences (positive and negative), then move into action and accountability.

FINAL THOUGHTS ...

If you had read the front page story of the *San Francisco Chronicle* on Thursday, December 14, 2005, you would have read about a female humpback whale that had become entangled in a spider web of crab traps and lines. She was weighted down by hundreds of pounds of traps that caused her to struggle to stay afloat. She also had hundreds of yards of line rope wrapped around her body, her tail and her torso as well as a line tugging at her mouth. A fisherman spotted her just east of the Farralone Islands (outside the Golden Gate) and radioed an environmental group for help. Within a few hours, the rescue team arrived and determined she was so bad off that the only way to save her was to dive in and untangle her, which was a very dangerous proposition. One slap of the tail could kill a rescuer.

They worked for hours with curved knives and eventually freed her. When she was free, the divers say she swam in what seemed like joyous circles. She then came back to each and every diver, one at a time, and nudged them. She pushed them gently around—she thanked them. Some said it was the most incredibly beautiful experience of their lives. The guy who cut the rope out of her mouth says her eye was following him the whole time, and he will never be the same.

A coach is not so different from the divers who freed the humpback whale. Good coaches work to help their clients "get untangled" from the things binding them.

Chapter Eight

Coaching and Conflict

All of those who work closely with individuals and teams find themselves, at one time or another, in the middle of conflict. Many leaders and coaches feel inadequately prepared for conflict. In our attempt to resolve the conflict, we may either unknowingly escalate the conflict or inadequately address the root cause of the issue, both of which do little to solve the conflict situation. As coaches we frequently find ourselves coaching individuals and groups around the topic of conflict.

Effective conflict is the key to preserving relationships and moving forward positively. When approached effectively, conflict can lead to better solutions, creativity and relationships. When approached ineffectively, conflict can destroy relationships, and impede and/or bring to a halt the resolution of issues.

In relationships, organizations and teams, conflict is inevitable, however, "combat" is optional. How we choose to "show up" in conflict situations will determine whether we participate in "conflict" or "combat."

Conflict is like "fire." When handled appropriately it is useful, positive and needed; when handled inappropriately or left unattended, conflict can easily and quickly destroy relationships, teams and organizations.

> SELF-AWARENESS is key to effective conflict. To approach conflict effectively we must be aware of our actions.
> Do you REACT or RESPOND?

Levels of Conflict

An important consideration when dealing with conflict is to remember it is a process; how we interact with that process will determine our conflict effectiveness.

Conflict occurs at different levels with different behaviors and perspectives. The levels of conflict include the following:

Level 1: DIFFERENCES

- See situation differently.
- Understand each other's differences/perceptions.
- No real discomfort.

Level 2: **MISUNDERSTANDING**

- What is she thinking?
- Doesn't understand differences.

Level 3: DISAGREEMENT

- Sees situation differently.
- Feels discomfort that the other person disagrees.

Level 4: DISCORD

- Discomfort in interaction, as well as issue.

Level 5: POLARIZATION

- Begin recruiting others to join the cause.

When coaching, it is important to determine at what level you, as a coach, will enter into the conflict, as well as how you will approach the situation. In level one, you may find yourself much less involved (if at all) than in levels two and three. In levels two and three, you will likely be more involved, with a particular emphasis on helping those involved see the situation clearly, differently and respectfully. In levels four and five, you will likely set clear expectations and will work to find common ground and regain respect.

I once worked with two internal teams who were in conflict, which led to an external issue with a key client. This team had managed to get to level four before they began to work with me. The first things that had to be re-established were expectations, ground rules and trust. The coaching that occurred initially was more focused and direct. Once the team began to regain some trust and open up, the coaching process became more fluid and flexible.

Conflict Styles and Approaches

Your conflict style, in large part, determines how you respond, coach and work within conflict. General approaches to conflict fall into the following styles:

- Win at all costs

- Peace at all cost

- Give in

- Split the difference

- Win/Win

Resolving conflict in a collaborative manner yields better results and maintains the relationship. Getting your way in the near term, at the expense of a relationship, usually results in a long-term loss. Conflicts are best resolved using collaboration, which maintains the relationship AND successfully resolves the issue.

As individuals with a diversity of backgrounds, family and perspectives, we all have our own individual approach to conflict. In that approach we also have "trigger" points that can surface conflict more quickly in each of us. An important component to effective conflict is to be self-aware of what triggers conflict in each of us individually. According to the authors of *Conflict Dynamic Profile*, there are nine typical conflict triggers:

> Your actions toward conflict send a message about how you handle conflict.

1. Unreliable

2. Overly analytical

3. Unappreciative

4. Aloof

5. Micro-managing

6. Self-centered

7. Abrasive

8. Untrustworthy

9. Hostile

Constructive ways of responding to conflict include:

- Focus on the facts, not on the person or our assumptions.
- Take a time out, step away and regroup.
- Examine your perspective by looking at pros and cons equally.
- Constructively express emotions.
- Respond versus react.
- Reach out, ask questions, and be open to the other perspective.
- Reflective thinking; examine your biases, preferences and blind spots.
- Adapt and be flexible.

Destructive ways of responding to conflict include:

- Winning at all costs.
- Displaying anger.
- Demeaning others.
- Retaliating and getting even.
- Avoiding the conflict situation and/or person(s) involved in the conflict.
- Yielding in a passive/aggressive manner.
- Hiding emotions.
- Self-criticizing.

Conflict **BENEFITS** include:

- Stimulates creativity/brainstorming.
- Improves teamwork.
- Encourages listening.
- Promotes reflective thinking.
- Yields new information.
- Signals change is coming.

Conflict **COSTS** include:

- Poor quality decisions.

- Poisons relationships.

- Disrupts productivity.

- Inhibits communication.

How You Show Up

Effective conflict involves listening to the other person, being open to new/different viewpoints and asking questions to gain perspective. In conflict situations, we need to constantly monitor our actions as well as other's actions to ensure we move forward appropriately. In effective conflict, HOW we approach the situation is equally (if not more) important to WHAT we do or say in our approach.

> INTENTION does not always equal our ACTIONS. We are judged by our actions not our intentions. Very rarely do we know with 100% accuracy other's intentions. Therefore, it is risky to assume ACTIONS = INTENTIONS.

When coaching conflict, a key consideration is how we show up prepared to interact in the situation. There are three main areas for consideration:

1. The first area is how YOU show up—how you personally decide to enter into the conflict—your attitude.

2. The second area is your approach to working it out. How do you view the conflict and subsequently work to resolve it—the task of resolving the conflict.

3. The final area is how you treat others in the process of resolving the conflict—the relationship side of resolving conflict.

    - **Listen.** Free from judgment and with an open mind.

    - **Choose your battles wisely.** Know when to go forward and when to walk away.

    - **Don't assume you know the facts.** Question and really listen to the answers, keep an open mind.

    - **Find common ground.** Work to find common ground and/or agreement and then start from that perspective.

How You Work It Out

- **Take a view from the other side of the fence.** Look at the situation objectively. Seek first to understand. When possible give yourself time to "cool off."

- **"Respond" versus "React."** Don't lose emotional control.

- **Take responsibility for your part of the conflict.** Own up to your part. Be honest, candid and ready to address your part.

- **Get to the root cause.** Ensure you understand the root cause, not just the surface issue.

- **Putting your standards on others.** Make sure you are respectful and strive to understand other's standards without imposing your standards on them.

How You Treat Others

- **Work your differences out in private.** Keep conflict between the person(s) involved, no audience needed.

- **Treat others respectfully.** Acknowledge the other person. Treat them how you would want to be treated.

- **People don't care how much you know until they know you care.** In conflict, "knowing that you care" could be the shift that takes the conversation toward resolution.

- **Win/Win.** Look for how everyone can come out with something positive.

- **Giving opposing messages.** Saying one thing and doing another. Conflicting verbals and non-verbals.

- **Hiding behind technology.** Using email, text, voicemails, etc., to avoid interaction.

In summary, remember that effective conflict can be a positive signal in the lives of those we coach, as it can improve relationships, support creativity and signal that shifts and breakthroughs are occurring to support forward movement. The key to using conflict to improve relationships is to remember to support effective conflict, not full on combat.

Chapter Nine

The Coaching Leader

Coaching is an important skill for those in leadership as they work with individuals and teams. The leader who coaches contributes to individual and team performance, provides developmental opportunities for those they lead, and supports a pathway for empowering others to move forward positively and successfully.

Coaching conversations can occur in various forms—during one-on-one sessions, in ad hoc meetings to problem solve issues and performance reviews, working with intact teams, as a tool for HR professionals and organizational leaders, or as a part of feedback conversations.

> Many of the world's most admired corporations, from GE to Goldman Sachs, invest in coaching. Annual spending on coaching in the US is roughly $1 billion.
> ~Harvard Business Review

John Whitmore, author of *Coaching for Performance: GROWing People, Performance and Purpose*, states that "a coach's main job is to create AWARENESS and invoke RESPONSIBILITY." Those equipped with strong coaching skills will grow as future leaders and be the "norm" in organizations that are effective and successful.

A study conducted by the Manchester Group found the following effects of good coaching, as referenced in the article *Return on Investment in Coaching Studies—11 Study Summary*:

- Improved Relationships – 77%
- Stronger Teamwork – 67%
- Job Satisfaction – 61%
- Productivity – 53%
- Quality – 63%

Jack Zenger, CEO of Zenger Folkman and author of several business leadership and coaching books, including *Results Based Leadership and the Extraordinary Coach: How the Best Leaders Help Others Grow*, conducted research on coaching and surfaced the following five important business outcomes:

When the manager is an *effective coach*:

1.   Employees are more productive and more likely to go the extra mile.

2.   Employees are more engaged, satisfied and committed.

3.   There is a high correlation between coaching and retention of employees.

4.   Employees believe they have the opportunity to grow and move forward.

5.   The feedback and relationship with their manager is more positive.

Coaching is a practical and tangible way to learn how to effectively lead. Coaching can be used to develop skills or solidify skills learned in training. Coaching adds value in the following ways:

*   **Individualized Approach.** Tailored to fit each individual.

*   **Targeted Approach.** Focused on addressing issues/concerns important to the individual.

*   **Sustainable Approach.** Not giving advice. This is about helping individuals find their answers and learn how to move forward with that knowledge.

*   **Results Driven Approach.** Holds individuals accountable to their actions and associated results.

As I talk with clients, I find individuals who participate in coach training share the following feedback about their learning and professional growth:

*   I really need to sharpen my listening skills and focus on deep listening.

*   I need to stop "consulting" (telling) and start "coaching" (asking).

*   I need to spend less time talking and more time listening.

*   I need to ask powerful questions that elicit awareness.

*   I need to quit giving advice and let others find the answers for themselves.

*   The coaching model is a guideline—it is a way for me to structure the conversation so that awareness is created and action and accountability is supported.

*   Accountability is the key to all conversations.

As I train leaders to use coaching, I often use the term "coach approach," which means incorporating coaching principles into your leadership style. When I first started my coach training, I quickly realized coaching skills would drastically change not only my approach to leading individuals, but also to building teams, parenting, communicating with others and even consulting. I quickly learned using a "coach approach" in all my interactions produced better results, more engagement and a higher level of accountability. What I discovered was a coach approach included the following:

- Setting the coaching agreement informally, by finding out the most important perspective or issue to discuss and then understanding the outcome desired.

- Listening deeply to both verbal and nonverbal communication.

- Being curious and asking questions that lead to awareness, discovery and forward action.

- Designing actions as well as structuring accountability and follow up to ensure forward progress is achieved.

While all eight building blocks are important, as a coaching leader, the following are key building blocks when using coaching as a leadership tool.

- The Coaching Agreement
    - What to discuss and outcome desired
- Powerful Questions
    - Discovery, awareness, forward action
- Deep Listening
    - For the coachee—verbals, non-verbals, tone, inflection, pace
    - For the coach—clearing your mind of distractions, eliminating multi-tasking both physically and mentally
- Creating Awareness
    - Distinctions, challenging limiting beliefs, false assumptions
- Action, Accountability and Follow up
    - Design the action, structure accountability and set follow up

As a coaching leader you will encounter situations that can be either "content rich" or "content free" environments, and your coaching will need to be adapted to be effective. Feedback and performance review discussions, as well as training, tend to be content rich environments, while developmental and problem solving discussions tend to be content free environments.

Content rich coaching generally refers to coaching in situations where there is a standard content base, such as curriculum, SOPs, statement of work, etc., and there are fixed roles and defined goals. In these situations you are coaching within already defined content.

When coaching in a content rich environment, you tend to coach from the listening, questioning, action and accountability perspective. Strong listening skills coupled with powerful questions are most effective. Frequently, the best approach is to ask questions from the content and then use your deep listening skills to understand the reactions and responses being shared. Listen for limiting beliefs and false assumptions and share your perspectives and observations. Lastly, utilize your action and accountability skills to ensure learning is implemented.

Content free coaching usually refers to situations where the content is minimal or virtually non-existent. Roles and goals are not clearly defined.

When coaching in a content free environment, it is important to establish the coaching agreement, plus the agreed upon results and take-away for the group. Then, continue with the coaching model.

Coaching versus Feedback

When coaching as a leader, it is extremely important to understand the distinction between coaching and feedback.

Coaching is the process of partnering with individuals and teams in a deliberate, creative, action-based manner to maximize potential, designing of actions, and personal action and accountability.

Feedback is usually one-sided and intended to offer advice, perspective and/or opinion on a particular situation, communication and/or goal. In most cases it is either a subjective response or evaluative data on past performance.

Coaching is:

- Future focused
- Enhancing existing skills
- Discovering challenges and opportunities
- Inquiry-oriented
- Asking the right questions

Feedback is:

- Past-focused

- Giving advice

- Evaluative in nature

- Corrective

- Telling and/or opinion-oriented

Both coaching and feedback are important in the workplace, but they are not the same. At times they are used in the same conversation, while at other times they are separate conversations. *The key to being an effective leader is to know when to coach, when to give feedback, and how and when to join coaching and feedback together.*

In performance reviews, a coaching approach can be utilized to enhance the effectiveness of the performance review. Most performance reviews are designed to provide feedback on performance over a certain period of time based on a set of competency guidelines.

A coach approach will increase the effectiveness of the performance review by empowering the individual receiving the performance review to become actively involved in the review and associated future action. The following process provides a guideline for incorporating coaching into performance review discussions.

STEP 1: Set Up the Performance Review Discussion.
Discuss how the process will work, what is in it for them, what you hope to achieve, the benefits of this type of discussion, and how this will support your working relationship going forward. Ask the individual what they want to accomplish in the performance review discussion.

STEP 2: Ask the Recipient for Their Perspective.
Send the performance review document to the individual ahead of time, ask them to review it, and to come prepared with questions and their perspective on the information contained in the review. Give them an opportunity at the BEGINNING of the meeting to discuss their perspective.

STEP 3: Use Deep Listening, Powerful Questions and Creation of Awareness Skills.
As the individual is giving their perspective, use your deep listening skills to really listen to what is being shared. Ask powerful questions. Look for ways to help them discover and become aware of key learnings. Really listen to what the individual is saying about their performance. Notice how the individual is internalizing and interpreting the data.

STEP 4: Provide Your Perspective on the Performance Review.
Give your perspective on the data provided, as well as any perspective on the individual's response. As you provide feedback, look for ways to communicate in a coach approach manner.

STEP 5: Discuss Gaps and Design Action.
Help the individual to consider the gaps and their desired goal. Support the individual in brainstorming and developing actions to move them forward and close the gap based on their desired goal.

STEP 6: Develop a Plan for Action, Accountability and Follow Up.
Discuss and confirm the actions to be implemented. Partner together on a plan for accountability and follow up regularly to ensure forward progress is taking place.

I am often asked "When should you NOT coach?" While coaching can be used very effectively in many situations, there are times when coaching will not be the most effective tool to use. Consider the following as signals that a coach approach may not be the best approach:

- Lack of skill or ability
- When forward progress is impeded by past issues
- No motivation or desire to move forward
- Specific feedback or direction is needed
- Disciplinary action is required

Chapter Ten

Individual and Group Coaching Lab

THREE-PRONGED LEARNING APPROACH

The coaching lab provides each participant an opportunity to deepen their coaching competency by using the skills in a real situation while being supervised. It is designed to provide a safe, constructive and real environment for individuals in coach training to practice their skills and receive feedback. Each person will have an opportunity to be the coach, coachee and the observer.

The coaching lab provides individuals with a three-pronged approach to learning:

- As the coach, you will be able to practice your skills in a real, live environment.
- As the coachee, you will have the opportunity to learn by experiencing coaching from the perspective of being coached.
- As the observer, you will have the opportunity to learn as you observe the coaching session in process.

WRITTEN FEEDBACK

There are two important reasons why written feedback is required.

1. To help the coach become a better coach.
2. To help the observer learn the "Eight Building Blocks of Coaching."

GIVING FEEDBACK

When sharing your observations and suggestions:

- Acknowledge the coach for actions or skills that moved the coachee forward.
- Praise successful coaching and specifically tell why it was successful.
- Point out valuable assets—such as a sense of humor—to the coach.

- Share with the coach areas needing improvement.

- Provide praise and tactful suggestions—in the same manner you would like to receive feedback when you are the coach.

- Avoid judgmental statements such as "You should have."

Resources

RESOURCE A: THE EIGHT BUILDING BLOCKS OF COACHING

This document is intended as a Quick Reference Guide and as a tool for review of the Eight Building Blocks of Coaching.

1. Deep Listening

Listening is defined as:

- Being curious about the other person.
- Quieting your own mind chatter so that you can be fully present with another person.
- Creating a safe space for someone to explore.
- Conveying value. You are important to me!
- Not about giving answers, but exploring possibilities.
- Reflecting back, like a mirror, what you experienced from the person.
- Really getting another person.

What to listen for:

- Listen within the context versus content only.
- Listen for values, beliefs, frustrations; what is said versus what is not said.
- Listen for limiting beliefs and false assumptions.

Challenges of listening:

- Quieting the mind or "mind chatter."
- Thinking about what to say next.
- Discomfort with silence.
- I'm too busy to listen.

2. Powerful Questions

One of a coach's greatest tools is the use of powerful questions. Powerful questions promote the exploration of new possibilities and stimulate creativity. They place the individual or team in a place of responsibility. They empower individuals and teams to consider what is right for them.

Powerful questions are:

- Directly connected to deep listening. Really getting what the other person is saying enables the coach to craft the most effective question.

- Brief. They are laser-sharp and to the point.

- Without judgment. There is no hidden agenda. They are not leading or suggestive.

- Usually open-ended. Promoting further conversation and gathering of information.

- They help clarify and slow down the automatic responses and thinking.

- Powerful questions invite us to shift our perspective.

What are the different types of questions?

- Questions that help the person gain perspective and understanding.

- Questions that evoke discovery.

- Questions that promote clarity and learning.

- Questions that call for action.

3. Artful Language

Language is the vehicle by which we express ourselves and help others do the same. Language has the potential to create a positive impact and propel us forward. Language also has the potential to derail and inflict great harm. Artful language includes an awareness and further development of our own language and an awareness of the other person's language.

Artful language includes:

- Word choices

- Alignment of language.

- Metaphors, stories and quotes

- Distinctions

- Acknowledging

4. Action and Accountability

Action and accountability play a significant role in coaching. One of the primary reasons that a person decides to work with a coach is that they want someone to help them take action and reach their goals. This part of the coaching process has several components: brainstorming, designing the action, and follow through.

Brainstorming includes:

- Helicoptering
- Defining the bull's-eye
- Identifying limiting beliefs and false assumptions
- Truth-telling
- Seeding
- Stretch

Designing the action involves:

- Baby steps
- Backward planning
- Doing it now

Follow-through is:

- Acknowledging
- Creating structure
- Strategizing
- Anchoring
- Designing "blitz days"
- Identifying daily action

5. Coaching Relationship

In coaching, the three most important things are: relating, relating and relating. The coaching relationship is the vehicle of change and transformation.

The benefits of relating well to someone include:

- The likelihood of success increases.

- Your effectiveness as a coach increases.

- The likelihood that a prospective coachee will want you to coach them increases.

Components of the coaching relationship are:

- Trust and intimacy

- Coaching presence

6. Coaching Agreement

The coaching agreement is comprised of both initial components and an ongoing nature. The ongoing nature of the coaching agreement includes:

- Helping the coachee gain clarity about what they want to focus on in that particular coaching session, as well as what they want to take away.

- As the coaching session unfolds, continuing to clarify and explore the take away throughout the coaching session.

- Holding side-by-side the initial need that brought them to coaching and the current focus/take-away. Because coaching is discovery-based, not outcome-based, new insights and perspectives need to be integrated into the coaching agreement.

- A check-in midway to later in the coaching session.

7. Creating New Awareness

Creating new awareness is about raising the blinds and letting in the light of additional information, perspective and intention. New awareness is fostered when:

- Curiosity is encouraged.

- Clarifying questions are raised.

- Beliefs and assumptions are articulated and verified.

- You intentionally walk to the other side of the room to gain a different perspective.

- You are open to other ways of viewing and interpreting the same situation.

New awareness is facilitated by:

- Listening on multiple levels.

- Contextual Listening.

- Drilling down.

- Listening for clues.

Eliminating limiting beliefs and false assumptions:

- What do you want to achieve?

- What might you be assuming that is stopping you from achieving your goal?

- Articulate the POSITIVE OPPOSITE of your limiting belief or false assumption.

- Ask the incisive question.

- Write down the action you will take.

8. Direct Communication

Direct communication is the ability to communicate effectively during the coaching process, using language that will have the greatest positive impact on the person being coached.

Characteristics of direct communication:

- Clear and laser-sharp.

- In the moment (timely).

- Constructive and judgment free.

- Appropriate silence and pauses. Authentic.

- Demonstrates a mastery of language.

- Does not stack questions.

- Does not step over things.

Four specific forms of direct communication include:

- Interrupting

- Advising

- Directing

- Messaging

RESOURCE B: COACHING EVALUATION FORM

Coaching Evaluation Form

Coaching4Today's Leaders

Coach:

Coachee:

Observer:

Date:

Directions: Use the *Eight Building Blocks Evaluation Form* as your guide for providing feedback to other coaches. Please share your comments and observations.

Eight Building Blocks of Coaching

1. DEEP LISTENING	• Listened without judgment, criticism or agenda.
	• Listened without thinking about what you will be saying next.
	• Listened for values, frustrations, motivation and needs.
	• Listened for the greatness in the person you are coaching.
	• Listened for limiting beliefs and false assumptions.
	• Listened for *shoulds*, *oughts* and *musts*.
	• Listened for the obvious.
	• Noticed the tone, pace, volume, inflection and frequently used words.

STRENGTHS

OPPORTUNITIES

2. POWERFUL QUESTIONS	• Promoted the exploration of new possibilities and stimulated creativity.
	• Placed coachee in the position of responsibility.
	• Empowered coachee to consider what is right for them.
	• Brief, laser-like and to the point.
	• Without judgment.
	• No hidden agenda.
	• Not leading or suggestive.
	• Usually open-ended.
	• Questions promoted further conversation and gathering of information.
	• Questions assisted in clarifying and slowing down automatic responses and thinking.
	• Questions provided a shift in perspective.

STRENGTHS

OPPORTUNITIES

3. ARTFUL LANGUAGE	• Used clean, neutral, non-manipulative and agenda-less language.
	• Used language that goes below the surface to the core issue(s).
	• Matched the words/phrases of the coachee and knew when to introduce new words.
	• Matched the pace and pattern of the coachee.
	• Used language to help coachee learn, describe their values and define their reality.
	• Intentionally aligned language to convey acceptance and that you "get them."
	• Intentionally misaligned language as a way of calling attention to a specific issue.

STRENGTHS

OPPORTUNITIES

4. ACTION AND ACCOUNTABILITY	• Helped coachee discover different perspectives and possibilities.
	• Encouraged coachee to rise above their current situation and see the bigger picture.
	• Helped coachee define what success looks like.
	• Raised awareness of new ideas and nurtured current ideas.
	• Challenged coachee to stretch themselves.
	• Assisted coachee in designing their actions with measurable outcomes.
	• Encouraged a "do it now" attitude.
	• Assisted coachee in developing an action plan.
	• Assisted coachee in identifying how they will stay focused on the task at hand.
	• Identified barriers that might derail forward progress.

STRENGTHS

OPPORTUNITIES

5. COACHING RELATIONSHIP	

5. COACHING RELATIONSHIP

- Provided a safe and supportive environment.
- Genuine concern was demonstrated.
- Provided a space for the coachee to be "real," where they can share, risk and explore without fear of judgment or rejection.
- Trust was modeled.
- Worked to go "deeper" with the coaching to the core issues.
- Provided their full attention to the coachee.
- In constant discovery mode.
- Open to not knowing and was comfortable "dancing" with the coachee.
- Used humor effectively.
- Did not get enmeshed in the coachee's issues and challenges.

STRENGTHS

OPPORTUNITIES

6. COACHING AGREEMENT

- Asked coachee to articulate their desire/goal for the coaching session.
- Used paraphrasing with coachee to ensure understanding.
- Helped coachee gain clarity about what they wanted to focus on during the coaching session.
- Asked coachee to define the "take away" they wanted from the coaching session.
- Further clarified and explored the "take away" throughout the coaching session.
- Was flexible in changing focus if conversation necessitated a change in direction.
- Held side-by-side the initial need that brought them to coaching and the current focus/take away.

STRENGTHS

OPPORTUNITIES

---

7. CREATING NEW AWARENESS	• Demonstrated and encouraged curiosity.
	• Used clarifying questions to further explore topics and uncover new insights.
	• Articulated, questioned and verified beliefs and assumptions.
	• Intentionally offered a new/different perspective for the coachee to consider.
	• Opened up other ways of viewing and interpreting the same situation.

STRENGTHS

OPPORTUNITIES

---

8. DIRECT COMMUNICATION	• Clear and laser.
	• In the moment (timely).
	• Authentic, constructive and judgment free.
	• Appropriate silence and pauses.
	• Did not stack questions.
	• Did not "step-over" issues/topics.
	• Interrupted appropriately and with respect.
	• When interrupting, asked for permission. *"May I interrupt you?"*

---

8. DIRECT COMMUNICATION	• Bottom-lined it for the coachee. *"Here's what I'm hearing..."*
	• Gave advice as an educated, experienced opinion only after all other options had been explored. *Here's what I've seen work. Tell me if it sounds like it's worth experimenting with.*
	• Re-focused or steered the coachee back toward their goals, when needed.
	• When appropriate, the coach reminded them of the importance of what they are doing and where they are going.
	• "Truth told"—coach told it like they saw it.
	• Acknowledged the coachee and tapped into their greatness.
	• Coach endorsed what the coachee had accomplished.
	• Advised them on what was next. *"You probably need to start focusing on ABC, because you've moved past XYZ."*
	• Coach told them what they wanted for them. *"What I want for you is..."*

STRENGTHS

OPPORTUNITIES

OVERALL COMMENTS

POSSIBLE OPPORTUNITIES FOR DEVELOPMENT

RESOURCE C: SAMPLE WELCOME KIT

Sample Welcome Letter

Welcome and Congratulations!!!

Thank you for deciding to begin the coaching process and for choosing me as your coach. My commitment is to provide you with the best possible coaching that I can.

In order for you to get the most out of your coaching sessions, I am sending you a number of items for you to read before your first coaching session. These items include:

- **A Coaching Agreement.** My request is that you read this contract, sign it and return it to me.

- **Contact information.** This information is kept private.

- **Code of Ethics.** I am a member of the International Coach Federation and I have signed an agreement to abide by their Code of Ethics.

- **First Coaching Session Form.** I ask that you complete and return this to me prior to your first coaching session.

- **Focus Report.** This is a quick and simple report that I ask you to complete and return to me prior to each coaching session (excluding your first coaching session). Completion of this form not only helps you prepare for each coaching session, but also prepares me as your coach.

At the time of the agreed upon coaching session, I ask you to call me at <**Enter Your Telephone Number Here**>. Each session is approximately 30 minutes in length. Since I have clients before and after each coaching session, it is important that we adhere to the 30-minute timeframe.

Occasionally, between coaching sessions, you may want to call or e-mail me. Please feel free to do either. My commitment is to respond to you in a timely manner, as time permits.

Again, welcome to the coaching process and congratulations on taking this important step forward.

<**Your Name Here**>

Sample Agreement

Coaching Agreement

To my client: Please review, adjust, sign where indicated, and return to me at the address listed below.

NAME

INITIAL TERM

FEE PER MONTH $

NUMBER OF SESSIONS PER MONTH

SESSION DURATION

REFERRED BY:

GROUND RULES:

> 1. CLIENT CALLS THE COACH AT THE SCHEDULED TIME.
>
> 2. CLIENT PAYS COACHING FEES IN ADVANCE.
>
> 3. CLIENT PAYS FOR LONG-DISTANCE CHARGES, IF ANY.

1. As a client, I understand and agree that I am fully responsible for my physical, mental and emotional well-being during my coaching calls, including my choices and decisions. I am aware that I can choose to cancel this coaching agreement at any time upon 30 days written notice.

2. I understand that "coaching" is a Professional-Client relationship I have with my coach that is designed to facilitate the creation/development of personal, professional or business goals and to develop and carry out a strategy/plan for achieving those goals.

3. I understand that coaching is a comprehensive process that may involve all areas of my life, including work, finances, health, relationships, education and recreation. I acknowledge that deciding how to handle these issues, incorporating coaching into those areas, and implementing my choices is exclusively my responsibility.

4. I understand that coaching does not involve the diagnosis or treatment of mental disorders as defined by the American Psychiatric Association. I understand that coaching is not a substitute for counseling, psychotherapy, psychoanalysis, mental health care or substance abuse treatment, and I will not use it in place of any form of diagnosis, treatment or therapy.

5. I promise that if I am currently in therapy or otherwise under the care of a mental health professional, I have consulted with the mental health care provider regarding the advisability of working with a coach and that this person is aware of my decision to proceed with the coaching relationship.

6. I understand that information will be held as confidential unless I state otherwise, in writing, except as required by law.

7. I understand that certain topics may be anonymously and hypothetically shared with other coaching professionals for training or consultation purposes.

8. I understand that coaching is not to be used as a substitute for professional advice by legal, medical, financial, business, spiritual or other qualified professionals. I will seek independent professional guidance for legal, medical, financial, business, spiritual or other matters. I understand that all decisions in these areas are exclusively mine and I acknowledge that my decisions and my actions regarding them are my sole responsibility.

I have read and agree to the above.

_____

Client Signature

Date:

Please return to:

_____

Sample Contact Form

Contact Information

*(Please forward this information to me at <**Enter Your Email Address Here**>)*

Name:

Address:

Telephone Numbers (best way to reach you):

Primary:

Secondary:

Other:

Email Address:

Would you like to receive my monthly e-newsletter?   Yes   No

Organization and your role:

Sample First Coaching Session Form

First Coaching Session

Please answer the following questions and e-mail your responses to me at least one day before your first coaching session.

1. What are 10 things I **absolutely** need to know about you and your organization?

1) _____

2) _____

3) _____

4) _____

5) _____

6) _____

7) _____

8) _____

9) _____

10) _____

2. What do you want to be able to say about yourself or your organization three months from now that you cannot currently say?

One year from now?

Three years from now?

Continued on next page...

3. Why is this important to you?

4. What is holding you back? What keeps getting in the way?

5. What is one simple thing you could do to get closer to your goal?
   (Right now! Today! This week!)

Sample Focus Report Form

Focus Report

Name: Date:

Please call <Enter Your Telephone Number Here> **for your coaching sessions.**

What I have accomplished OR what action I have taken since our last session:

What I did not accomplish but intended to do AND what got in the way:

At this moment, the biggest challenges or issues I am dealing with are:

I want to focus our attention during our next coaching session on:

RESOURCE D: A LIST OF POWERFUL QUESTIONS

Top 10 Year-End Questions for You or Your Team

1. What have you accomplished this year? Be specific. Write it down. Schedule some time to celebrate this!

2. What have you learned this year? What skills did you pick up? What lessons?

3. What got in your way? Where will your work be next year? Be honest if it was you who got in the way.

4. Who contributed to your success? What can you do to recognize these members of your personal or professional team?

5. What mistakes did you make, and what did you learn from them? Writing these down is a good refresher for what not to do next year.

6. How was your work consistent with your values?

7. Where did you not take responsibility? Sometimes this is easier to see with a little distance from the actual event.

8. How did your performance rate? Give yourself a letter grade or a 1 to 10 score.

9. What do you need to let go of? Doing so can help you move much more lightly into the New Year.

10. What was missing for you this year? How can you incorporate it into next year?

Top 10 Questions for Leaders

1. What do you want to be able to say three years from now that you can't say today (about yourself or your organization)?

2. What are the possible next steps?

3. Who can help you with this?

4. What's the truth about now?

5. How do you handle failure?

6. What do you model?

7. How much of a people pleaser are you?

8. What do you need to say goodbye to in order to move forward?

9. On a scale of 1 to 10 how committed are you to taking action? (1= no commitment, 10=high commitment)

10. What's the payoff of not taking action?

Favorite Questions

1. What's next?

2. What do you want?

3. What are you afraid of?

4. What is this costing you?

5. What are you attached to?

6. What is the dream?

7. What is the essence of the dream?

8. What is beyond this problem?

9. What is ahead?

10. What are you building towards?

11. What has to happen for you to feel successful?

12. What gift are you not being responsible for?

13. What are your healthy sources of energy?

14. What's stopping you?

15. What's in your way?

16. What would make the biggest difference here?

17. What are you going to do?

18. What do you like to do?

19. What can you do to be happy right now?

20. What do you hope to accomplish by having that conversation?

21. What do you hope to accomplish by doing that?

22. What's the first step?

23. What would it be like to have excitement and fear at the same time?

24. What's important about that?

25. What would it take for you to treat yourself like your best client?

26. What benefit/payoff is there in the present situation?

27. What do you expect to have happen?

28. What's the ideal?

29. What's the ideal outcome?

30. What would it look like?

31. What's the truth about this situation?

32. What's the right action?

33. What are you going to do?

34. What's working for you?

35. What would you do differently?

36. What decision would you make from a place of abundance?

37. What other choices do you have?

38. What do you really, really want?

39. What if there were no limits?

40. What aren't you telling me that's keeping me from coaching/helping you?

41. What haven't I asked that I should ask?

42. What needs to be said that has not been said?

43. What are you not saying?

44. What else do you have to say about that?

45. What is left to do to have this be complete?

46. What do you have invested in continuing to do it this way?

47. What is that?

48. What comes first?

49. What consequence are you avoiding?

50. What is the value you received from this meeting/conversation?

51. What is motivating you?

52. What has you hooked?

53. What is missing here?

54. What does that remind you of?

55. What do you suggest?

56. What is underneath that?

57. What part of what I said was useful? And how so?

58. What is this person contributing to the quality of your life?

59. What is it that you are denying yourself right now?

60. What do you need to put in place to accomplish this?

61. What is the simplest solution here?

62. What would help you know I support this/you completely?

63. What happened?

64. What are you avoiding?

65. What is the worst that could happen?

66. What are you committed to?

67. What is your vision for yourself and the people around you?

68. What don't you want?

69. What if you knew?

70. What's your heart telling you? What are you willing to give up?

71. What might you have done differently?

72. What are you not facing?

73. What does this feeling remind you of?

74. What would you do differently if this problem were solved?

75. What does your soul say?

76. What do you need to say goodbye to in order to move forward?

77. What's the payoff for you of not dealing with this issue?

78. Are things as bad as you say they are or are they worse?

79. At what point when you say "yes" are you really feeling "no"?

80. What is the decision you are avoiding?

81. What are you pretending not to know?

82. What are ten things I absolutely need to know about you?

83. What do you want to be able to say about yourself three months from now? One year from now? Three years from now?

84. What is holding you back? What keeps getting in the way?

85. What is one simple thing you could do today to get you closer to your goal? (Right now! Today!)

86. What is your biggest, wildest dream?

87. What keeps you up at night? What do you find yourself continually thinking about when you're in the shower?

88. What has motivated you in the past to reach/achieve difficult goals, make important decisions, or do challenging things? Can we use this as a motivator now?

89. Who can help you with this?

90. What are you tolerating?

91. What has served you in the past? Is it still in effect now?

92. What would you do if you knew you couldn't fail?

93. What part of this goal is yours? What belongs to someone else? What if the goal was all yours?

94. How can I best support you? What do you need most from me?

95. What are you grateful for?

96. What makes your heart sing?

97. What's missing?

98. What do you have to do differently to make this happen?

99. What do you need to put in place to make this happen?

100. When you attain your goal, what will it look like?

101. Who do you know that is already doing this well?

102. What will be the signs that it's time to begin?

103. How will you know that you have succeeded?

104. How will you know when you arrive?

105. What about yourself—do you need to change?

106. What is one thing you need to focus on to get where you want to go?

107. Could you be mistaken? How could you check this out?

108. Does this align with your vision and goals?

109. What is one thing you feel really good about over this past week?

110. What one thing would make the biggest difference right now?

111. What's your belief about this situation?

112. What would you like more of? Less of?

113. What is true about this situation?

114. What are the effects of this on you?

115. What steps would move this forward?

116. How attached are you to the outcome?

117. What is the "should" in this situation?

118. Is this the time to begin?

119. What is the truth about this situation?

120. What is the path of least resistance?

121. Is there another way? Let's brainstorm five to ten other possibilities.

122. What is this costing you?

123. Can you see what is beyond this problem?

124. Can you see what's ahead?

125. Are you open to a completely different way of looking at this?

126. What are your actions saying about this situation?

127. What will happen if you keep doing this for the next ten years?

128. Underneath all of this, what are you really committed to?

129. What is the legacy that you want to leave behind?

130. May I push you on this?

131. So, what's possible here?

132. What opportunities are you not taking advantage of?

133. Who's really in charge here?

134. What are five changes or actions that you can take in the next 30 days that will move you forward?

135. What are you willing to do to make this work?

136. What consumes your time, to the point that it distracts you from attaining your goals?

137. What do you really, really, really, REALLY want?

138. What are you afraid of about this situation?

139. What is the worst that could happen? And if that happened, what's the worst that could happen after that?

140. What is the best that could happen?

141. What are you NOT saying? What are you holding back?

142. Are you pursuing a goal that no longer makes sense?

143. What internal rules and unspoken standards are having a negative impact?

RESOURCE E: ADDITIONAL COACHING TECHNIQUES AND STRATEGIES

We've included in this text a number of exercises and techniques that you can use in your coaching.

Focus Exercise

This exercise helps the individual gain clarity about their primary roles and responsibilities.

Begin by writing your responses to each of these questions:

- What are the things that only you can do?
- What are the things that you and others can do?
- What are the things that you can do, but choose not to do?
- What are the things that you cannot do and never want to do?

Look over your answers and deepen your learning with these additional questions:

- How does what you have written compare with how you actually spend your time and energy?
- What would it take to spend the majority of your time doing what only you can do?
- Who do you need to be in order to make this a reality?

Identify the changes and adjustments necessary and take action now. Today.

Leadership Timetable

In order to respond to the challenges of leadership, leaders must make time for these priorities:

- **Rest:** Every good leader understands the importance of taking care of their physical body. (Also see Power Sabbath below.)
- **Results:** Make time for your main goals.
- **Response:** Make sure there is adequate time for follow-up and follow-through.
- **Refocus:** Schedule time for course corrections and fine-tuning.

Ask your coachees which of the four "Rs" they frequently forget. The final "R" is often the most overlooked. Then ask "Which of these "Rs" would be of the greatest benefit to you and your leadership?"

The 4 Rs

The four areas of rest include:

1. **Physical Rest:** Make sure your body is getting adequate rest.

2. **Mind Rest:** Enjoy some silence. Turn off the TV. Take a break from reading the depressing news in the paper. Just let your mind rest.

3. **Heart Rest:** Caring for others and their needs can become exhausting. Take a short break and let others care for you. You'll be better able to care for others when you return.

4. **Soul Rest:** Take time to experience the silence. Rest in the knowledge that the world does not revolve around you or me!

When traveling by airplane, we're reminded that, in an emergency, those traveling with children are to put on their own oxygen mask first and then care for their children. A strong personal foundation is like putting on your oxygen mask first. You are then better able to care for and lead those around you.

Split Time Versus Solid Time

A common challenge among coaching clients is getting things done, especially those items that only they can do. The to-do list keeps growing. Feelings of guilt and inadequacy take root. The latest technological gizmos are of no assistance. No matter what, there still aren't enough hours in the week to do all you want and need to do.

If you look more closely at your tasks and what they require, you can get past this bottleneck in no time. You see, some tasks require a solid block of time to be completed. These items often require a creative flow of thought or have a sequence/strategic process to them. Every time you stop and re-start a solid block project, you lose valuable time and momentum.

Split-time tasks, on the other hand, can be stopped and restarted with little to no loss of time or momentum. These kinds of tasks can be worked on when you discover a few extra minutes or when you're on auto-pilot.

Give this a try: Begin by identifying what you need to do in any given week. Then, for each task, decide if you need a "solid" block of time OR a "split" block of time.

You will be amazed at how this simple distinction will allow you to use your time so much more efficiently, and how much more quickly you will complete the tasks on your list.

References

Capobianco, S., Davis, M., and Kraus, L. *Conflict Dynamics Profile.* St. Petersburg, FL: Eckerd College Leadership Development Institute, 1999.

Capobianco, S., Davis, M., and Kraus, L. *Good Conflict, Bad Conflict: How to Have One Without the Other.* Mt. Eliza Business Review, Summer-Autumn 2005.

Covey, Stephen. *The 7 Habits of Highly Effective People.* London: Simon & Schuster, 1999.

Crum, Thomas. *The Magic of Conflict: Turning a Life of Work into a Work of Art.* 2nd ed. Touchstone, 1998.

Deutschman, Alan. *Change or Die: The Three Keys to Change at Work and in Life.* HarperCollins, 2007.

The International Coach Federation, http://www.coachfederation.org.

Kline, Nancy. *Time to Think.* London: Cassell Illustrated, 1999.

Leeds, Dorothy. *Smart Questions.* McGraw-Hill, 1987.

Lim, Evelyn. "Our Life Journey: Break Free From Limiting Beliefs — Abundance Tapestry." Love Yourself, Love Your Life. May 29, 2008. http://www.abundancetapestry.com/break-free-from-limiting-beliefs.

McGovern, PhD, Joy, and Michael Lindemann, PhD. "Maximizing the Impact of Executive Coaching: Behavioral Change, Organizational Outcomes, and Return on Investment." The Manchester Review , Vol. 6, No. 1 (2001)

Mayer, Bernard S. *The Dynamics of Conflict Resolution: A Practitioner's Guide.* San Francisco: Jossey-Bass Publishers, 2000.

Pawlik-Kienlen, Laurie. *Protecting Personal Boundaries.* 2006.

Runde, Craig E., and Tim A. Flanagan. *Becoming a Conflict Competent Leader: How You and Your Organization Can Manage Conflict Effectively.* 2nd ed. San Francisco: Jossey-Bass Publishers, 2012.

Scholtes, Peter R., et al. *The TEAM Handbook.* Madison, Wisconsin: Oriel, Inc., 2003.

Scott, David Meerman. *World Wide Rave: Creating Triggers that Get Millions of People to Spread Your Ideas and Share Your Stories.* Hoboken, NJ: JohnWiley & Sons, Inc., 2009.

Stull, Craig, Phil Myers and David Meerman Scott. *Tuned In.* New Jersey: John Wiley & Sons, Inc., 2008.

Van Sant, Sondra S. *Wired for Conflict: The Role of Personality in Resolving Differences.* Gainesville, Florida: Center for Applications of Psychological Type, Inc., April 2003.

Weiss, Jeff, and Jonathan Hughes. "Want Collaboration? Accept – and Actively Manage – Conflict." Harvard Business Review. March 1, 2005. http://hbr.org/2005/03/want-collaboration-accept-and-actively-manage-conflict/ar/1

Weiss, Jeff, and Jonathan Hughes. "Want Collaboration? Accept—and Actively Manage—Conflict." Harvard Business Review. http://hbr.org/2005/03/want-collaboration-accept-and-actively-manage-conflict/ar/1.

Winesman, Albert L., Donald O. Clifton, and Curt Liesveld. *Living Your Strengths: Discover Your God-Given Talents and Inspire Your Community.* New York: Gallup Press, 2003-2004.

Zander, Rosamund Stone and Benjamin Zander. *The Art of Possibility: Transforming Professional and Personal Life.* London, England: Penguin Books, Ltd., 2000.

Zenger, John H., David Ulrich, and W. Norman Smallwood. *Results-Based Leadership.* Boston: Harvard Business School Press, 1999.

Zenger, John H., and Kathleen Stinnett. "The Extraordinary Coach: How the Best Leaders Help Others Grow." Harvard Business Review Press. April 15, 1999.

About the Authors

Dr. J. Val Hastings, MCC, is the Founder and President of Coaching4Today'sLeaders, Coaching4Clergy, Coaching4Groups, and Coaching4BusinessLeaders. Val hired his first coach while he was pastoring at a local United Methodist church. His progress was noticeable by all, and he began to wonder, "What if I adopted a coaching approach to leadership?" In that moment, a vision began to emerge—a global vision of Every Leader a Coach.

Dr. Hastings is the author of numerous books and has developed four coach training programs which are accredited and approved to the highest level by the International Coach Federation. These trainings are offered globally and are offered in many languages, including English, Spanish, Portuguese, and Korean. Graduates of these programs have received all three coaching credentials: ACC, PCC, and MCC.

Val currently holds the designation of Master Certified Coach through the International Coach Federation, its highest coaching designation. He also holds the designation of Professional Mentor-Coach. In addition to teaching at his own programs, Val holds faculty status at Coach University and Faith Evangelical Seminary. In 2006, Val was a presenter at the global gathering of the International Coach Federation and, in 2007, he served as the President of the Philadelphia ICF Chapter.

Trigena H. Halley, PCC, is the founder and owner of Peak Performance CCT, LLC, which she started in 2009 as a way for her to combine her 20+ years of organizational consulting experience with professional coaching. During her professional career, Trigena has held various leadership positions in the global corporate arena, with a focus on talent development, execution of strategy, achievement of financial goals and client satisfaction.

She specializes in leadership coaching, performance improvement, development of leaders, and working with organizations to employ a sustainable culture of performance and results. Her experience spans service, non-profit, manufacturing, corporate, educational and faith-based organizations. Trigena has significant experience training and coaching groups. She has led the development and implementation of large-scale leadership and coach training programs for several global corporate clients. She also offers a wide variety of individual and organizational assessments.

Trigena is a Professional Mentor-Coach and holds the designation of Professional Certified Coach through the International Coach Federation.

Passionate about the great outdoors, Trigena leads experiential leadership programs and women's adventure retreats using the sport of canyoneering. These adventures provide a rich forum for realization of individual potential. She has found nature itself provides the ideal palate for learning and change.

In 1999, Trigena moved to Sandy, Utah, where she spends four seasons a year outdoors—skiing, hiking, running, river rafting and canyoneering slot canyons. She continues to explore the great state of Utah and other exciting destinations with her husband, two children, and friends.

Made in the USA
Middletown, DE
30 August 2017